The

Abingdon Worship
Annual 2017

CONTEMPORARY &
TRADITIONAL
RESOURCES FOR
WORSHIP LEADERS

Abingdon Worship
Annual 2017

Edited by
Mary J. Scifres
and B.J. Beu

Abingdon Press / Nashville

The Abingdon Worship Annual 2017

CONTEMPORARY AND TRADITIONAL RESOURCES
FOR WORSHIP LEADERS

Copyright © 2016 by Abingdon Press

This book is printed on acid-free paper.

ISBN 978-1-5018-1093-0

16 17 18 19 20 21 22 23 24 25—10 9 8 7 6 5 4 3 2 1

MANUFACTURED IN THE UNITED STATES OF AMERICA

Contents

December

Indexes

Online Contents

The following materials are found only in the Abingdon Worship Annual 2017 section at www.abingdonpress.com/downloads. Instructions on how to view these materials in your browser or download them to your computer are available at the site. PLEASE NOTE: This file is password protected (see page 288).

Introduction

Worship brings us into God's presence in a unique and blessed way. Preparing to lead others in worship is both a joyous honor and a solemn undertaking. Wouldn't it be wonderful if we had uninterrupted time each week to devote to this sacred task? Some weeks, worship is front and center in our lives and in our minds. More often than not, though, worship planning is squeezed among a myriad of other tasks and responsibilities. Some weeks, worship planning falls to the bottom of our task list.

Still, the people gather to be fed and to connect to the holy each week in worship. And so, worship leaders need to offer prayers, prepare an order of worship, select music, and even prepare a sermon. Into that weekly task, we offer this resource to strengthen your ability to lead creatively and prepare consistently.

Following the Revised Common Lectionary, *The Abingdon Worship Annual 2017* provides theme ideas for each liturgical day and the written and spoken elements of worship to allow congregations to participate fully in the liturgical life of worship. (Those who seek assistance with visuals and multimedia resources that many worship services require will find what they are looking for in Mary's online resource, *Worship Plans and Ideas*. Visit http://maryscifres.com and click on Resource Subscriptions for more details.)

For basic song and hymn suggestions, as well as for online access to the hard copy materials, we include internet access for each worship service at abingdonpress.com/downloads (see p. 288 for instructions on accessing the download). The PDF format allows users to import printed prayers and responsive readings directly into bulletins for ease of use and printing. In addition to the hymn and song suggestions, the online link includes some bonus material: suggested hymns and entries for additional special days (New Years' Day, Ascension Day, All Saints' Day, and Thanksgiving).

In *The Abingdon Worship Annual 2017*, you will find the words of many different authors, poets, pastors, laypersons, and theologians. Some authors have written for this resource before, while others provide a fresh voice. Since the contributing authors represent a wide variety of denominational and theological backgrounds, their words will vary in style and content. Feel free to combine or adjust the words within these pages to fit the needs of your congregation and the style of your worship. (Notice the reprint permission for use in worship given on the copyright page of this book.)

Each entry provides suggestions that follow an order of service that may be adapted to address your specific worship practice and format. Feel free to reorder or pick and choose the various resources to fit the needs of your worship services and congregations. Each entry follows a thematic focus arising from one or more of the week's scriptures to fit the Basic Pattern of Christian Worship—reflecting a flow that leads from a time of gathering and praise, into a time of receiving and responding to the Word, and ending with a time of sending forth; each includes Centering Words, Call to Worship and Opening Prayer, Prayer of Confession and Words of Assurance, Response to the Word, Offertory Prayer, and Benediction. Communion resources are offered in selected entries. Additional ideas are also provided throughout this resource. Please note that Centering Words may be printed in a worship handout or projected on a screen. Use the words offered here in the way the best suits your congregation's spiritual needs, and please remember to give copyright and author credit!

Using the Worship Resources

Centering Words and Calls to Worship gather God's people together as they prepare to worship. Often called "Greetings" or "Gathering Words," these words may be read by one worship leader or responsively. Regardless of how they are printed in this resource, feel free to experiment in your services of worship. They may be printed for reflection, read antiphonally (back and forth) between two readers or two groups within the congregation: women and men, choir and musicians, young people and old, and so on.

Opening Prayers in this resource are varied in form, but typically invoke God's presence into worship. Whether formal, informal, general, or specific, these prayers serve to attune our hearts and minds to God. Although many may be adapted for use in other parts of the worship service, we have grouped them into the category "Opening Prayers."

Prayers of Confession and **Words of Assurance** lead the people of God to acknowledge our failing while assuring us of God's forgiveness and grace. Regardless of how they are printed, whether unison or responsively, Prayers of Confession and Words of Assurance may be spoken by a single leader or led by a small group. Some prayers may even be used as Opening or Closing Prayers.

Litanies and **Responsive Readings** offer additional avenues of congregational participation in our services of worship. Think creatively as you decide how to use these Responsive Readings in your service of worship: in unison, by a worship leader alone, or in a call-and-response format. Feel free to change the title of these liturgies to sit your worship setting.

Benedictions, sometimes called "Blessings" or "Words of Dismissal" send the congregation forth to continue the work of worship. Some of these Benedictions work best in call-and-response format, others work best when delivered as a blessing by a single worship leader. As always, use the format best suited to your congregation.

Although you will find *The Abingdon Worship Annual 2017* an invaluable tool for planning worship, it is but one piece of the puzzle for worship preparation. For additional music suggestions, you will want to consult *Prepare! An Ecumenical Music and Worship Planner*, or *The United Methodist Music and Worship Planner*. These resources, available through http://www.cokesbury.com, contain lengthy listings of lectionary-related hymns, praise songs, vocal solos, and choral anthems. For video, screen visual, and secular songs, along with experiential worship ideas for each Sunday, subscribe to Mary Scifres Ministries' online resource *Worship Plans and Ideas* at http://maryscifres.com/Worship_Subscription.html.

As you begin your worship planning, read the scriptures for each day, then meditate on the **Theme Ideas** suggested in this resource. Review the many words for worship printed here and listen for the words that speak to you. Trust

God's guidance and enjoy a wonderful year of worship and praise!

Mary J. Scifres and B. J. Beu, Editors
The Abingdon Worship Annual
beuscifres@gmail.com

Learn more about workshop and training opportunities through Mary Scifres Ministries at http://www.maryscifres.com.
If you find yourself in Southern California, come visit us at our Top of the World Retreat home, or visit B. J. at Neighborhood Congregational Church (www.ncclaguna.org).

January 1, 2017

First Sunday after Christmas

Mary J. Scifres

Color

White

Scripture Readings

Isaiah 63:7-9; Psalm 148; Hebrews 2:10-18; Matthew 2:13-23

Alternate Readings for New Year's Day/Watch Night

Ecclesiastes 3:1-13; Psalm 8; Revelation 21:1-6a; Matthew 25:31-46

(See online supplemental materials for a complete New Year's Day/Watch Night entry.)

Theme Ideas

Throughout Matthew's birth narrative, God's angels and messengers guide and protect Joseph and Mary on their journey into parenthood. Messages come to Joseph and Mary through angels, through dreams, and even through visitors from far away. Messengers and angels guide, shelter, and serve as a conduit for God's wisdom.

Listen for God's messages in today's readings and tune your ear to hear the many messengers that come your way in this holy season and in the year ahead.

Invitation and Gathering

Contemporary Gathering Words (Matt 2)

Surely God's presence is with us—in the brush of an angel's wings, in the radiance of a newborn child, in the wisdom of a visitor, in the message of a friend. Listen. God is speaking. Look. God is here.

(Begin or end Gathering Words or Centering Time by singing "Surely the Presence of the Lord.")

Call to Worship (Matt 2)

Gathered here, we listen for God.
God's angels are all around us.
Gathered here, we look for signs of God's presence.
God's presence is with us now.
Gathered here, we celebrate the birth of Christ.
God comes in the gift of a child.

Opening Prayer (Matt 2)

Holy One, speak to us in dreams.
Visit us with your angels,
and guide us with your messengers,
that we may hear their truth
and share their wisdom.
Open our minds, our hearts, our ears, and our eyes
to recognize your guidance
and to walk in your ways.

Proclamation and Response

Call to Confession (Matt 2)

Voices of sorrow haunt our world. Cries of desperation touch our hearts and disturb our thoughts. Bring your sorrows and your hopes, as we come before God to confess our deepest need.

Prayer of Confession (Matt 2)

Mighty God, bearer of our burdens,
>you know the demons that haunt our minds;
>you know the sorrows that burden our hearts.
Send your angels and messengers of peace
>to comfort and guide us.
Help us follow in the footsteps of Joseph and Mary—
>listening, learning, and following
>>where you would have us go.
And save us from the path of Herod—
>rejecting your guidance,
>destroying the hope that you send,
>causing others to weep in anguish.
Send angels and messengers of peace
>to comfort and guide us.
Send your mercy and grace
>to reconcile and restore us,
>>that we may be carried into the arms
>>>of your mercy.
In hope and gratitude, we pray. Amen.

Words of Assurance (Heb 2)

Christ has set us free from our fears,
>from our sins, and even from death.
Rejoice and be glad, for the Christmas message is this:

Christ is born in our world and in our hearts.
In Christ, we are forgiven and free!

Passing the Peace of Christ (Heb 2)
Proclaim Christ's presence, here and now, by sharing
Christ's peace with signs of love and joy.

Introduction to the Word (Matt 2)
Listen, for angels may be speaking.
Listen for the message that God is sending.
Look for the dreams that God is dreaming.

Response to the Word (Ps 148)
Praise the Lord, messengers of God.
Praise God, sun and moon.
Praise God, angels of heaven and earth.
Praise the Lord, messengers of God.
Praise God, all the earth.
**Praise God with the messengers of God
all around us.**

Thanksgiving and Communion

Invitation to the Offering
Bring praise, bring hope, bring open hearts...for God
calls us to share our gifts and offerings with the world.

Offering Prayer (Isa 63, Matt 2)
Holy God, send your Christmas message
of love and peace through these offerings.
May our offerings, our ministries, and our lives
be like angels of hope.
May they save those who are in distress
and comfort those who weep.
In your blessed name, we pray. Amen.

Sending Forth

Benediction (Isa 63, Matt 2)
Go as God's angels, with messages of peace.
Go as God's angels, with messages of hope.
Go as God's angels, with messages of love.
We go forth with the angels of God.

January 6, 2017

Epiphany of the Lord

Mary J. Scifres

Color

White

Scripture Readings

Isaiah 60:1-6; Psalm 72:1-7, 10-14; Ephesians 3:1-12;
Matthew 2:1-12

Theme Ideas

The radiance of Christ shines throughout the Epiphany readings each year. The power of Christ's radiance emanates for all the world to see. The brightness of Christ's presence shines upon every person in every nation. The radiant star of Matthew 2 shines so brightly that sages could follow its guiding light for miles and miles; and two thousand years later, Christians are still drawn to this light, as we decorate our trees and light our candles. The radiance of Christ shines upon our Epiphany celebration, calling us to follow God's guiding light.

Invitation and Gathering

Centering Words (Isa 60, Matt 2)

The light of Christ is shining…shining for all to see. The light of Christmas is glowing…glowing in our homes and in our hearts. The light of God is guiding us…guiding us to follow the light that came to earth on Christmas.

Call to Worship (Isa 60, Matt 2)

A star shines brightly to bring light for all to see.
Shine in our world, Christ Jesus.
A star shines brightly to guide our journey.
Shine in our lives, Christ Jesus.
A star shines brightly to call us together this day.
Shine in our worship, Christ Jesus.
Shine, Jesus, shine.

Opening Prayer (Isa 60, Matt 2)

Light of the World, shine upon us
as we worship you.
Draw us to your manger of light,
that we might see your radiant presence.
Guide us with your holy light,
that we might walk in your ways.
Shine in and through us,
that we might be people of your radiant love,
leaving footprints of light
with every step we take.
In Christ's name, we pray. Amen.

Proclamation and Response

Prayer of Confession (Matt 2)

As we kneel at your manger,

we acknowledge that we rarely humble ourselves
before you.
As we meditate upon the Christmas star,
we confess how seldom we slow down
to look for your guidance.
Correct our neglectfulness.
Heal our shortcomings,
and forgive our sins.
As you shine upon us with your mercy and grace,
guide us back to your path
and draw us ever closer to you.
In the light of your love, we pray. Amen.

Words of Assurance (Isa 60)

Arise, for you are forgiven!
Shine, for you are loved!
God's glory and grace
shine upon us with forgiveness and love.

Passing the Peace of Christ (Isa 60)

As forgiven, beloved children of God, let us be signs of
light and love as we share the peace of Christ together.

Prayer of Preparation (Isa 60)

Radiant God, source of all illumination,
shine through the words of scripture this morning.
that we might see your face
and hear your wisdom;
shine through our hearts and minds,
that we might know your truth
and see your guiding light;
shine through our lives and actions,
that we might radiate your light and love,
in all that we say and in all that we do.

Thanksgiving and Communion

Invitation to the Offering (Matt 2)

Come with your gifts—gifts of gold, frankincense and myrrh. Come with your gifts—gifts of light, hope, generosity, and love. Come with the gifts we have received from God—gifts great enough for Christ!

Offering Prayer (Isa 60, Matt 2)

Radiant Christ, shine through these gifts,
    that your love may shine through them
        for all the world to see and follow.
Shine through our lives,
    that your love may shine through us
        for all the nations to perceive and embrace.

The Great Thanksgiving

The Lord be with you.
    And also with you.
Lift up your hearts.
    We lift them up to the Lord.
Let us give thanks to the Lord our God.
    It is right to give our thanks and praise.
It is right, and a good and joyful thing,
    always and everywhere to give thanks to you,
    Almighty God, creator of heaven and earth.
From the dawning of creation,
    you have brought forth light to guide our ways.
From ancient times, you have guided us
    with burning bushes, pillars of fire,
    flashes of lightning, and the light of each new day.
When we turned from your light
    and walked in darkness, you called us back,

delivering us from the depths of despair
and reclaiming us as children of light.
And so, with your people on earth,
and all the company of heaven,
we praise your name
and join their unending hymn, saying:
Holy, holy, holy Lord, God of power and might,
heaven and earth are full of your glory.
Hosanna in the highest. Blessed is the one
who comes in the name of the Lord.
Hosanna in the highest.
Holy are you and blessed is your Son, Jesus Christ.
In the fullness of time, you sent Christ,
the Light of the World, to shine upon us anew,
and to bless us with love, grace and light.
Through Christ's light and love,
you rescue us from darkness,
and call us "good."
Through Christ's light and love,
those first disciples were gathered together
in the midst of their brokenness,
were reclaimed by Christ,
and were blessed by his glorious light
in the breaking of the bread
and the sharing of the cup.
And so we come into that light,
remembering how Jesus took bread,
gave thanks to you, broke the bread,
gave it to the disciples and said,
"Take, eat; this is my body, which is given for you.
Do this in remembrance of me."

We come to this table,
>   remembering how Jesus took the cup,
>   gave thanks to you, gave it to the disciples
>   and said, "Drink from this, all of you;
>   this is my life in the new covenant, poured out
>   for you and for many for the forgiveness of sins.
>   Do this, as often as you drink it,
>   in remembrance of me."
And so, in remembrance of these
>   your mighty acts of light and love,
>   we offer ourselves in praise and thanksgiving
>   as children of light,
>   in union with Christ, the Light of the World,
>   as we proclaim the mystery of faith.
>   **Christ has died.**
>   **Christ is risen.**
>   **Christ will come again.**

Communion Prayer
>   Pour out your Holy Spirit on us
>   and on these gifts of bread and wine.
>   Make them be for us the life and love of Christ,
>   that we may be for the world the body of Christ—
>   the Light of the World—
>   redeemed by Christ's love
>   and reclaimed by your grace.
>   By your Spirit, make us one with Christ,
>   one with each other,
>   and one in ministry with the world,
>   until Christ comes in final victory
>   and we feast at the heavenly banquet.
>   Through Jesus Christ,
>   with the Holy Spirit in your holy Church,
>   all honor and glory is yours, Almighty God,
>   both now and forevermore. **Amen**.

Giving the Bread and Cup
(The bread and wine are given to the people, with these or other words of blessing.)
The light of Christ, shining in you.
The love of Christ, shining through you.

Sending Forth

Benediction (Isa 60)
Arise, shine!
Christ's light has come.
Arise, shine!
Christ's light shines through us.
Arise, shine, for all to see!

January 8, 2017

Baptism of the Lord

Rebecca J. Kruger Gaudino

Color

White

Scripture Readings

Isaiah 42:1-9; Psalm 29; Acts 10:34-43; Matthew 3:13-17

Theme Ideas

This Sunday's readings depict God doing the unexpected. God's voice, full of strength and majesty, disrupts creation (Psalm 29), calls God's servants "to open blind eyes, to lead the prisoners from prison" (Isaiah 42:6-7), and claims Jesus as God's own Son. Acts suggests that this God disrupts our lives, especially when we think we have Jesus' "message of peace" figured out (Acts 10:36). Peter and his Jerusalem colleagues discover that they are the blind, the ones sitting in darkness. Their settled sense of who and what is acceptable to God is shaken and shattered, like the wilderness and cedars of Psalm 29. God's majesty and strength, exemplified in Jesus Christ, promise (and threaten) unfettered power, even in our lives.

Invitation and Gathering

Centering Words

Washed in the waters of Christ's baptism, we are healed in the waters of love. Cleansed in the waters of God's Spirit, we are reborn in the waters of life. *(B. J. Beu)*

Call to Worship (Ps 29, Matt 3, Acts 10)

(Have the baptismal font front and center. Hold up a big pitcher of water and say the words. Then slowly pour the water into the font. During this pouring, have someone softly and slowly play a drumroll on a low-pitched drum.)

This is the living water of baptism—

a water that makes us new.

God's voice calls from this water—

a water that offers us new vision and purpose.

Listen for this voice!

—Or—

Call to Worship or Litany of Praise (Ps 29, Matt 3)

(Use the drumrolls of a low-pitched drum throughout the call to worship, letting the intensity of the drumming rise and fall where appropriate. These drumrolls could be part of the reading of the psalm and gospel as well.)

One:	God's voice calls from the waters.
Right:	*God's voice is strong and majestic.*
Left:	**Our glorious God thunders!**
One:	God's voice shakes the wilderness and shatters the cedars.
Right:	*God's voice is strong and majestic.*
Left:	**Our glorious God thunders!**

One: God's voice calls out to Jesus,
as he rises from the waters,
"This is my Son whom I dearly love!"

Right: *God's voice is strong and majestic.*

Left: **Our glorious God thunders!**

All: *Give glory and power to God! Amen.*

Opening Prayer (Ps 29, Isa 42, Acts 10)
Glorious God, Ruler enthroned over all,
you stretched out the heavens
and gave life and breath
to all who walk upon the earth.
In your glorious might,
bless us and strengthen us
with peace and justice.
Astonish us with your power, O God,
through Jesus Christ,
who was baptized by John
that we might be baptized,
and through the Holy Spirit,
who alighted like a dove upon Jesus
and who alights upon all who are baptized
in Jesus' name. Amen.

Proclamation and Response

Prayer of Confession (Ps 29, Isa 42, Acts 10)
God of strength and majesty,
bless us with your peace today.
When our worship is insincere
and we fail to do what is right,
forgive us.
Call us with your life-shaking voice,

and lead us from darkness
into the waters of your light and grace.
Work new miracles in our lives,
that we may be your sons and daughters,
in whom you delight—
even as Jesus was your delight
at his baptism. Amen.

Words of Assurance (Acts 10)
Long ago, Peter preached that everyone who believes
in Jesus Christ receives forgiveness of sins
through his name.
Peter's voice continues to echo today.
Rejoice in this message of forgiveness and peace!

Passing the Peace of Christ (Acts 10)
God shows no partiality to one group over another!
Brothers and sisters, we are all welcomed into this community of the baptized. Greet your neighbors in the peace
of Christ.

Prayer of Preparation (Ps 29, Isa 42, Matt 3, Acts 10)
Voice of God, you are powerful enough
to shake the wilderness,
yet tender enough to bathe Jesus in your love
at his baptism.
Tell us what you will bring about
through the gift of your Spirit
as your word falls upon us this day. Amen.

Response to the Word (Isa 42, Ps 29, Matt 3, Acts 10)
Glorious God, Ruler enthroned over all,
your voice thunders over the waters of chaos,
bringing order and peace.
But your voice also thunders
over places of order and peace,

uprooting our certitude
and shaking our settled lives.
Open us to your fresh possibilities,
that the blessing of our baptism
may reveal your Son's good news
through the outpouring
of your Holy Spirit. Amen.

Thanksgiving and Communion

Invitation to the Offering (Acts 10)
Jesus Christ came to proclaim a message of peace to all
people: All are loved by God. Let us give generously out
of this Christian longing for peace.

Offering Prayer (Isa 42, Matt 3, Acts 10)
Jesus Christ, baptized by John,
anointed by the Holy Spirit,
endowed with power for the healing of all,
use us and our gifts
to bring new life to our world. Amen.

Sending Forth

Benediction (Ps 29, Isa 42, Matt 3, Acts 10)
God's voice thunders over the waters.
and beckons from the waters of our baptism.
Sons and daughters of God,
listen for this voice—
a voice that interrupts and disrupts our lives,
a voice that leads us into newness of life.
God's Spirit is upon *us*!
Live in the blessing and calling of this power! Amen.

January 15, 2017

Second Sunday after the Epiphany
Hans Holznagel

Color

Green

Scripture Readings

Isaiah 49:1-7; Psalm 40:1-11; 1 Corinthians 1:1-9; John 1:29-42

Theme Ideas

Life and faith are so often lived in between moments of waiting. God acts, Jesus is born, the wise and the royal visit, and again (or still?) we wait, look forward, anticipate. Today's lections suggest active, creative, communal, even mystical waiting. And when the wait is finally over, they invite us to testify and to act.

Invitation and Gathering

Centering Words (1 Cor 1)

Grace and peace. Jesus has been born. Wise and royal visitors have come. Wait now for more to be revealed—revealed in prayer, in word, in warm welcomes.

Call to Worship (Ps 40)
>Happy are those who place their trust in God,
>who sing God's praise with a new song.
>>**God's wondrous deeds are many and great.**
>>**Their number is greater than the stars in the sky.**
>Happy are those who wait patiently for God,
>who cry out to God with their whole heart.
>>**For God hears our pleas**
>>**and listens to our requests.**
>God is steadfast and faithful.
>>**Let us worship the One for whom we wait.**

Opening Prayer (Ps 40, Isa 49, John 1)
>Transforming God, leader of life's journeys,
>>teach us what we need to learn—
>>>the ways and graces,
>>>>of creative, active waiting;
>>>the cry and the confidence
>>>>of the psalmist;
>>>the honest testimony
>>>>of the prophet;
>>>the clarion vision and the voice
>>>>of the mystic.
>Labor may sometimes seem in vain,
>>yet surely you are present;
>>surely you are here to deliver.
>Grant us eager hearts,
>>that we may delight to do your will. Amen.

Proclamation and Response

Prayer of Confession (1 Cor 1, John 1)
>O God, we find it hard to wait.

A good work done, a season accomplished,
 a list completed, a celebration:
  these we love,
   and we ask your blessings
    be upon them.
Yet we know more deeply
 that the wait is never completely over.
Your reign has come,
 and yet we wait for you
  to be more fully revealed.
Strengthen us in this, we pray,
 and help us to wait faithfully.
Sharpen our knowledge, bless our spirits,
 enhance our vision and ready us for action. Amen.

Words of Assurance (1 Cor 1)
 God is faithful.
 All who are called by God, and all who call upon God,
  will be strengthened, not blamed.
 In Christ Jesus, all are loved and forgiven. Amen.

Response to the Word (Ps 40)
 May all who seek, rejoice.
  Great is our God!
 O God, you are our help and our deliverer.
  May your will be done,
  and may we delight in doing it. Amen.

Thanksgiving and Communion

Offering Prayer (Ps 40, 1 Cor 1, Isa 49)
 Sacrifices and offerings you do not desire, O God,
  but the transformation of our hearts and minds.

This we know.
As we await your revelation in the world,
    fashion us and all that we offer this day
        into a living testimony of your glory. Amen.

Sending Forth

Benediction (Ps 40, 1 Cor 1)
    Go forth with open ears and eyes,
        awaiting the ongoing revelation of Jesus.
    May God strengthen you, guide your steps,
        and put a new song in your heart.
    Go in peace. Amen.

January 22, 2017

Third Sunday after the Epiphany

Mary J. Scifres

Color

Green

Scripture Readings

Isaiah 9:1-4; Psalm 27:1, 4-9; 1 Corinthians 1:10-18; Matthew 4:12-23

Theme Ideas

Light emerges in many different ways, bringing clarity and focus. For the Corinthian church, a renewed focus on Christ and Christ's teachings was needed to bring unity and to re-form community. Isaiah reminds his sister and brother Israelites of their call to be a light to the nations, helping them find a focused hope during a troubled time of exile. Similarly, Jesus calls the first disciples in response to these prophetic words of Isaiah. As light shines in the cloudy, confusing places of our lives, these words and stories can clarify our focus and help us answer God's call.

Invitation and Gathering

Centering Words (Isa 9, Matt 4)
Light shines. Light calls. Light guides our way. Focus on the light of Christ; answer the call and follow where Christ leads.

Call to Worship (Isa 9, Ps 27, Matt 4)
Christ is our light, our way in the dark.
Come to the light of Christ.
Christ calls us here, to worship and to pray.
Come and answer Christ's call.
Christ leads us forth, to teach and to heal.
Come and worship our God!

Opening Prayer (Isa 9, 1 Cor 1, Matt 4)
Light of the World, shine upon us this day.
Break through the clouds
    that separate us from one another,
        that we may worship you as one body.
Guide our steps,
    that we may walk in your light
        and live as your people of love.

Proclamation and Response

Prayer of Confession (Ps 27, 1 Cor 1)
You are our light, our salvation,
    the stronghold that lifts us up.
When our light dims from division and anger,
    shine upon us with your grace.
When our light fades from confusion and doubt,
    encourage us with your hope.

When our light recedes behind sin and regret,
 heal us with your mercy and truth.
O, that we would no longer walk in darkness,
  that we would cease to be divided from you
   and from one another.
In your face, we see a great light in our darkness.
In your love, we are unified
 and made one with you,
  one with each other,
   and one in ministry to the world.
In your grace, we become people of light.
May it be so.
May it be so. Amen.

Words of Assurance (Ps 27, Matt 4)

God is our light and our salvation.
In Christ, we no longer walk in darkness or division,
 but are called forth to unity and love,
  to light and life.

Passing the Peace of Christ (1 Cor 1)

I encourage you, sisters and brothers: Agree with one another. Let us break down the walls that divide us; and let us share together signs of peace with unity and love.

Introduction to the Word (1 Cor 1)

Christ's message may sound foolish in a world of death and despair, for Christ's message brings life and salvation. Christ's call may seem impossible in a world of shadow and cloud, but Christ's call opens us to God's light. May Christ's message and call strengthen our journey this day.

Response to the Word (Isa 9, Matt 4)

When you call, O God,
 we will listen.

As you teach,
> **we will focus.**
Where you lead,
> **we will follow.**
Guide us on your path,
> **and lead us into your light!**

Thanksgiving and Communion

Invitation to the Offering (1 Cor 1)
> United in mind and purpose, let us share in the ministry
> of generous giving this day.

Offering Prayer (Isa 9, 1 Cor 1, Matt 4)
> With these gifts,
>> bring justice to the oppressed
>>> and food to the hungry.
> With our ministry of love,
>> proclaim unity in a divided world.
> Bless us and bless these gifts,
>> that your light may shine
>>> in places shadowed by despair.

Sending Forth

Benediction (Isa 9, Ps 27, Matt 4)
> Go forth, with the light of Christ.
>> **Christ is our light, our way in the dark.**
> Go forth to answer Christ's call.
>> **Christ leads us forth, to teach and to heal.**

January 29, 2017

Fourth Sunday after the Epiphany

B. J. Beu

Color

Green

Scripture Readings

Micah 6:1-8; Psalm 15; 1 Corinthians 1:18-31; Matthew 5:1-12

Theme Ideas

God values humility, gentleness, justice, and mercy above displays of personal piety and social approval. The wisdom of the world, the power and strength of personal success—these are to be scorned in favor of the blessings that come from humility, peacemaking, and righteous living. Those who love God are called to do justice, love kindness, and walk humbly with their God.

Invitation and Gathering

Centering Words (Mic 6, Ps 15, 1 Cor 1, Matt 5)
Who is able to stand in the face of the storm and not be moved? Who is able to kneel before the Lord and not be put to shame? Those who walk blamelessly and speak

truthfully with gentleness from their whole heart. Those who are not afraid to appear foolish in the pursuit of peace.

Call to Worship (Mic 6, Ps 15, 1 Cor 1, Matt 5)
What does the Lord require of you?
To do justice, love kindness,
and walk humbly with our God.
With what shall we come before the Lord?
With speech that is gentle,
and words that build up.
With actions that bring peace,
and works that lift up the lowly.
Come, let us worship the Lord our God
in spirit and in truth.
All are welcome here!

Opening Prayer (Mic 6, Ps 15, 1 Cor 1)
Let the hills hear your voice, O Lord,
let the mountains quake before you.
Let all who call on your name
walk in the ways of righteousness and peace.
Let all who look to you for help
be blameless and do what is right.
May our words be gentle
and may our hearts be free from guile and deceit.
May our actions be rooted in justice and mercy,
and may we be known as peace makers,
the blessed children of God. Amen.

Proclamation and Response

Prayer of Confession (Mic 6, Ps 15, 1 Cor 1, Matt 5)
Holy One, we often feel beaten down by the world.
Numbed by our sorrow and grief,

we seek blessings for ourselves
rather than for those you call us to serve.
Wounded by careless words,
we lash out in our suffering
and hurt the very ones we love.
Weary of seeming weak and foolish,
we forsake humility and gentleness
and seek approval from those who need us
to be peacemakers and bridge builders.
Bless us, Holy One,
that we might be a blessing for others.
Fill us with a hunger and a thirst for righteousness,
that we may be pure in heart, merciful and kind,
and walk humbly in your ways. Amen.

Words of Assurance (Mic 6, Matt 5)
The God who blessed us to be a blessing
is stronger than our weaknesses,
and greater than our failings.
Even when we fall short,
God's love embraces us
and sets us on our feet again.

Passing the Peace of Christ (Matt 5)
Blessed are the peacemakers, for they shall be called
children of God. As God's beloved children, let us share
the peace of Christ with those around us.

Response to the Word (Mic 6, Matt 5)
What does the Lord require of you?
To do justice, love kindness,
and walk humbly with our God.
Blessed are the poor in spirit,
for theirs is the kingdom of heaven.

Blessed are the meek,
for they will inherit the earth.
Blessed are those who hunger and thirst
for righteousness, for they will be filled.
Blessed are the pure in heart,
for they will see God.
Blessed are the peacemakers,
for they will be called children of God.

Thanksgiving and Communion

Invitation to the Offering (Mic 6)
With what shall we come before the Lord? Will the Lord
be pleased with thousands of rams, with ten thousands
of rivers of oil? What does the Lord require of you but
to do justice, and love kindness, and to walk humbly
with your God? Then again, think how much good this
church could do with thousands of rams and ten thousands of rivers of oil! Will the ushers come forward to
receive today's offering?

Offering Prayer (Mic 6, Matt 5)
God of mercy and compassion,
    may these offerings be for the world:
        peace and justice,
        love and kindness,
        comfort and hope;
    may these offerings be for our church:
        honor and openness,
        gratitude and thankfulness,
        inspiration and expectation.
Blessed are those who seek justice, love kindness,
    and walk humbly with our God.

Sending Forth

Benediction (Mic 6, Ps 15, Matt 5)
Seek justice and discover God's blessings.
We go forth to walk humbly before our God.
Practice kindness and touch Christ's presence within.
We go forth to follow the way of peace.
Share mercy and abide in the Holy Spirit.
We go forth in the footsteps of compassion.

February 5, 2017

<u>Fifth Sunday after the Epiphany</u>
Laura Jaquith Bartlett

Color

Green

Scripture Readings

Isaiah 58:1-9a, (9b-12); Psalm 112:1-9 (10); 1 Corinthians 2:1-12, (13-16); Matthew 5:13-20

Theme Ideas

Light is an excellent theme as we finish out the Sundays after Epiphany and prepare to go up the mountain to experience the glow of Transfiguration. But today's scriptures are not about twinkling stars or shining faces. Isaiah, the psalmist, and Matthew—all connect light with the radiance of God's justice. We are called to be the light in acts of justice-making: feeding the hungry, clothing the poor, sheltering the homeless, freeing the oppressed. In these activities we shine God's light into the world. And it is here that we join together in joyful praise as we live in the light!

Invitation and Gathering

Centering Word (Isa 58, Matt 5)

Wanted:	*Light-Shiners*
Application Deadline:	*Always Open*
Job Description:	*Feed the hungry,*
	clothe the poor,
	shelter the homeless,
	free the oppressed.
Salary & Benefits:	*Living in God's light.*

—Or—

Centering Words (Isa 58, Matt 5)

God's Light is all around us...calling us forward, warming us...beckoning us into God's kingdom. Its demands are justice and mercy, compassion and grace. God's Light is all around us...calling us forward, warming us...leading us home. *(B. J. Beu)*

Call to Worship (Isa 58, Matt 5)

Voice 1:	Shout the good news aloud.
Voice 2:	Proclaim the good news with acts of justice.
All:	**Then our light will break forth like the dawn!**
Voice 1:	You are the light of the world.
Voice 2:	Shine God's light in your good works.
All:	**Then our light will shine forth for all people to see!**

(This would work especially well with the song, "We Are Called" ("Come, Live in the Light)" by David Haas, found at #2177 in The Faith We Sing.*)*

Opening Prayer (Isa 58, Matt 5)
>God of Justice, you call us
>>to shine the light of your abundance
>>>into our world.
>Equip us, we pray,
>>to feed those who hunger for bread
>>>and thirst for love.
>God of Compassion, you call us
>>to shine the light of your grace
>>>into our world.
>Inspire us, we pray,
>>to include the lonely, the marginalized,
>>>and the friendless in our circle of fellowship.
>God of Liberation, you call us
>>to shine the light of your joy
>>>into our world.
>Free us, we pray, from our fears,
>>that we might enter into joyful service
>>>and join in your dance
>>>>as we live in your light! Amen.

Proclamation and Response

Prayer of Confession (Isa 58, Matt 5)
>Dear God, over and over again,
>>you have taught us how to walk in your light.
>But we have sought to hide under a bushel,
>>hoping you won't notice
>>>how we avoid your radical call
>>>>to share our food with the hungry
>>>>>and our lives with those in need.
>You ask us to join your great dance of light,

33

but we are reluctant to associate
>with those we judge to be unworthy.
God, open our eyes to the joy of your justice—
>a justice intended for all the world.
Forgive our tendency to hide,
>our slowness to respond.
Invite us once more, O God,
>into the warmth of your light,
>>that we might shine brightly
>>>with your love. Amen.

Words of Assurance (Isa 58:11)
Hear these words of comfort and assurance
>from the prophet Isaiah:
>"The Lord will guide you continually
>>and provide for you, even in parched places.
>[The Lord] will rescue your bones.
>You will be like a watered garden,
>>like a spring of water that won't run dry."

Passing the Peace of Christ (Matt 5)
As you share the peace of Christ with one another, turn
to each person and say, "You are the light of the world!"

Response to the Word (Isa 58, Matt 5)
When we share food with the hungry...
>**we are the light of the world!**
When we care for those who are homeless...
>**we are the light of the world!**
When we offer companionship to the lonely...
>**we are the light of the world!**
When we clothe the poor...
>**we are the light of the world!**
When we speak up for justice...
>**we are the light of the world!**

When we do such things in a weary world...
we are the light of the light!

Thanksgiving and Communion

Offering Prayer (Isa 58, Matt 5)
Generous God, you shower us with blessings
and call us to share.
Thank you for this opportunity
to shine your light into the world
through our work of justice and compassion.
We pray and live in the name
of your true light, Jesus Christ. Amen.

Sending Forth

Benediction (Isa 58, Matt 5)
You are the light of the world!
Now take that light into all the places
that need the light and love of God.
Take that light into all the places
that need the light and grace of Jesus Christ.
Take that light into all the places
that need the light and inspiration
of the Holy Spirit.
Go and *be* the light of the world!

February 12, 2017

Sixth Sunday after the Epiphany

B. J. Beu

Color

Green

Scripture Readings

Deuteronomy 30:15-20; Psalm 119:1-8; 1 Corinthians
3:1-9; Matthew 5:21-37

Theme Ideas

Today's scriptures invite us to choose life and walk in
the ways of abundance. Moses urges the Hebrew people
to choose life; the psalmist praises those who walk in
God's ways; Jesus calls for a deeper, more faithful understanding of God's laws; and Paul reminds us that
God provides the growth that comes from choosing life.

Invitation and Gathering

Centering Words (Deut 30)

God invites us to choose life this day. Could it really
be that simple? Could the vast majority of our uncer-

tainties, our insecurities, our gut-wrenching angst fade away if we simply decided to choose life today? The hardest things in life are the least complicated. Choose life.

Call to Worship (Deut 30, Ps 119, 1 Cor 3)
Happy are those who walk blamelessly before God.
Blessed are those who walk in God's ways.
Happy are those who seek God with pure hearts.
**Blessed are those who take shelter
in God's teachings.**
Happy are those who come together in unity.
Blessed are those who choose life.

Opening Prayer (Deut 30, Ps 119, 1 Cor 3)
Bless us, Holy One, with your guidance.
Lead us in the ways that lead to life.
Teach us your statutes,
    and illuminate our path,
        that we may not stumble
            or be put to shame.
Speak to us once more
    your words of life,
        and feed us with spiritual food,
            that we may grow strong in faith
                and deep in loving kindness. Amen.

Proclamation and Response

Prayer of Confession (Deut 30, 1 Cor 3, Mark 5)
Loving God,
    when we turn from your ways
        and pursue paths of destruction,

> call us back to you once more
> and set our feet on right paths;
> when we choose sides
> and forsake our bonds of unity,
> call us together once more,
> and bind us with your Spirit.
> Feed us with the milk of your grace,
> and the spiritual food of your holy love,
> that we may grow strong as Christ's disciples
> and set aside the squabbles
> that challenge our unity. Amen.

Words of Assurance (Deut 30, 1 Cor 3)
> Happy are we when God answers our call.
> Blessed are we when we set our hearts on God.
> Choose life this day and live.

Passing the Peace of Christ (Deut 30, 1 Cor 3)
> Choose life, and you will find peace. Choose unity, and
> you will discover that our differences make us stronger,
> not weaker. In unity and holy love, choose life this day,
> as you share the peace of Christ with one another.

Response to the Word (Deut 30, Matt 5)
> Choosing life sounds like such an easy thing to do,
> yet it always ends up being difficult.
> Choosing life means letting go of our resentments.
> It means forgiving the injuries we have received.
> It means taking the high road.
> It means we are called to be better,
> that we may receive the blessings
> that true life bestows.

Thanksgiving and Communion

Invitation to the Offering (Deut 30, 1 Cor 3)
> Our very lives are a gift from God. What we do with that gift is up to us. Will we choose to embrace the life given? Will we share the blessings we have received with others? The choice is ours. But it is in giving that we receive, and it is in sharing that we taste the fullness of life. With grateful hearts, let us offer back to God our gifts this day, that others may be blessed through our giving.

Offering Prayer (Deut 30, Ps 19, 1 Cor 3)
> God of blessing, you have fed our faltering spirits
>> with the milk of your grace,
>>> and nurtured our wounded hearts
>>>> with the spiritual food of your healing love.
> May the gifts we bring before you this day
>> be signs of our commitment to choose life,
>>> as we walk in your ways
>>>> and grow united in your Son, Jesus.
> May the offering we share with a hurting world
>> bring the blessings of life
>>> and the happiness of friendship. Amen.

Sending Forth

Benediction (Deut 30, Ps 119)
> Happy are we when we walk blamelessly before God.
> **Blessed are we when we walk in God's ways.**
> Happy are we when we seek God with a pure heart.
> **Blessed are we when we take shelter
> in God's teachings.**
> Happy are we when we come together in unity.
> **Blessed are we when we choose life.**

February 19, 2017

Seventh Sunday after the Epiphany

Mary J. Scifres

Color

Green

Scripture Readings

Leviticus 19:1-2, 9-18; Psalm 119:33-40; 1 Corinthians 3:10-11, 16-23; Matthew 5:38-48

Theme Ideas

The Golden Rule of Leviticus 19:18 runs through all of today's readings. Living into this commandment to love others as we would be loved and to care for others with compassion is sometimes call the "law of love." Today's readings make clear that this is God's law. The path of love and compassion is the path of walking in God's ways. This is the foolishness of God to which we are called: the temple that we are building in our own lives and in the life of the church is to be a temple of love.

Invitation and Gathering

Centering Words (Lev 19, 1 Cor 3)

Love is the gift that calls us here. Love is the gift that makes us whole. Love is the gift that unites us with Christ and with one another.

Call to Worship (1 Cor 3)

Called here to God's temple, you are the temple of God.
We are the temple of love.
Called here to worship, you are the people of God.
We are the children of God.
Called to be love, you are a holy people.
We gather in the holiness of God's love.

Opening Prayer (Lev 19, Ps 119)

Holy God, make us holy with your grace
and fill us with your love.
Gather us together in your Spirit
and teach us your ways,
that we may live your law of love.

Proclamation and Response

Prayer of Confession (Lev 19, 1 Cor 3)

Holy One, you know we are not perfect.
Even as we hear you calling us to be your temple,
our minds wander and pull us away.
Even as you build us up to be your church,
we are torn down by division and disagreement.
Even as you set us upon the foundation of Christ Jesus,
we falter and find our feet on shifting sand.

41

Cover our imperfections with your mercy,
    and place our feet on the solid ground
        of Christ's grace and compassion.
Establish your law of love in our church and in our lives,
    that we may be the temple of love
        you create us to be.

Words of Assurance (1 Cor 3)
Don't you know that you are God's temple,
    and that God's Spirit lives in you?
You are! The Spirit lives within you!
The grace of Christ covers us all
    and creates us anew in forgiveness and love.

Passing the Peace of Christ (Matt 5)
With love and grace, let us greet one another in peace.

Prayer of Preparation (Lev 19, Ps 119, Matt 5)
Teach us, O God, the way of your love.
Speak to us in these words,
    and reveal yourself in this community.
Lead us onto the path of compassion
    and the way of your law of love.

Response to the Word (Matt 5)
Be perfect, as our heavenly God is perfect.
    Imperfect we come, to be perfected by God.
Be filled with love, as the Spirit is filled with love.
    Empty we come, to be filled by the Spirit.
Be full of grace and mercy, as Christ is full of grace
and mercy.
    We come needing grace,
    and grace leads us home.
Christ Jesus, show us the way!
    Christ Jesus, show us the way!

Thanksgiving and Communion

Invitation to the Offering (Matt 5)
> As our minds open to love, we discover that loving our neighbor means caring for strangers and sharing even with adversaries. With minds open to love, let us give generously to those in need.

Offering Prayer (1 Cor 3, Matt 5)
> By your grace, loving Christ, make these gifts holy.
> Transform each dollar into a sign of love,
>> each coin into the face of hope,
>>> and each prayerful gift
>>>> into a blessing of compassion.
> By your grace, loving Christ, bless this offering
>> as an offering of love.

Invitation to Communion (1 Cor 3, Matt 5)
> This table is not mine.
> This table is not yours.
> **This table is Christ's feast of love.**
> This church is not mine.
> This church is not yours.
> **This church is Christ's community of love.**
> As a community of love,
> we are welcomed to Christ's feast of love.
> **We come in Christ's mercy and grace.**

Sending Forth

Benediction (Matt 5)
> Go now in the perfect love of Christ Jesus,
>> strengthened by the power of the Holy Spirit
>> and led by the love of God.

Go to be perfect in love
through the grace of Christ Jesus,
who leads the way!

February 26, 2017

Transfiguration Sunday

James Dollins

Color

White

Scripture Readings

Exodus 24:12-18; Psalm 99; 2 Peter 1:16-21; Matthew 17:1-9

Theme Ideas

God blesses us with high points in life partly so that we can bear the low points. Like mountain peaks that attract our eyes and lift up our heads, God's blazing light shines for Moses on Mount Sinai and later through Jesus at the Transfiguration. In both cases, an unforgettable vision will help God's sojourners find strength for the trying journeys ahead. First Peter includes a unique first-person account of the Transfiguration, while Psalm 99 strikes a fitting chord of awe and praise. May the mountaintops of this Sunday strengthen us to traverse each valley with courage as we move into Lent.

Invitation and Gathering

Centering Words (Matt 17)

Transfigured by light, Jesus was changed. James, John and Peter saw it and were changed. Come away to the mountaintop; be still, be yourself, be who God intends you to be. Be changed.

Call to Worship (Ps 99)

Extol the Lord our God,
and worship at God's mountain.
For the Lord our God is holy,
full of compassion and grace.
When God's prophets cried out, God answered them,
speaking in a pillar of cloud.
Let all God's people sing praises
to God's great and awesome name.
Mighty God, lover of justice, you establish equity
throughout the earth.
Let us worship at God's holy mountain,
for the Lord our God is holy.

Opening Prayer (Matt 17, 1 Pet 1)

Light of God, shine upon us this hour.
We bring to you all that we are—
both our strengths and our weaknesses.
We lift our prayers for your world
in all its beauty and its pain,
trusting in your Spirit's power to redeem.
As your light once made Jesus appear radiant
on a mountaintop with Moses and Elijah,
transform us as we worship here today.

Let us encounter your Holy Spirit,
　　undeniably present among us,
　　　　that we may bear Christ's light
　　　　　　to a world that longs for peace. Amen.

Proclamation and Response

Prayer of Confession (Exod 24, Matt 17, 1 Pet 1)
　　Gracious God, we have seen your light and glory:
　　　　in the work of your church,
　　　　in the faces of loved ones,
　　　　　　and in the life of Jesus Christ.
　　Yet our memories are short,
　　　　and we soon start complaining
　　　　　　that you feel far away.
　　Forgive us when we descend from life's mountaintops
　　　　only to quickly forget how you have loved us.
　　Pardon us for the times we have neglected to seek you
　　　　in the faces of lonely or suffering neighbors.
　　Open our eyes and our ears, Lord.
　　Teach us to seek you and to listen as you call.

Words of Assurance (Exod 24, Matt 17, 1 Pet 1)
　　The light of God's grace shines upon us and through us.
　　Knowing us completely, God accepts and loves us.
　　In the name of Jesus Christ, we are forgiven. **Amen.**

Response to the Word (Matt 17)
　　Precious Lord, let us walk with you
　　　　as you have walked with us.
　　May we follow your Spirit to new mountaintops,
　　　　through low valleys,
　　　　　　and even to the cross.

May we follow your Spirit to new life,
through the grace of Jesus Christ,
now and forevermore. Amen.

Thanksgiving and Communion

Offering Prayer (Exod 24, Matt 17)
Dear God, Source of light and love,
all things belong to you.
You generously share with us
the blessings of home, food, friends,
and life itself.
Receive a portion of what you have given us
in our morning's offering.
May our gifts and joyful service strengthen your church,
that we may share good news and compassion
with those in need. Amen.

Sending Forth

Benediction (Exod 24, Matt 17, 1 Pet 1)
Let us not linger too long on this mountaintop.
Go and bear God's light
to a world that longs for peace.
May God our Creator, Redeemer, and Comforter
walk with us now and forevermore. **Amen.**

March 1, 2017

Ash Wednesday
B. J. Beu

[Copyright © 2016 by B. J. Beu. Used by permission.]

Color

Purple

Scripture Readings

Joel 2:1-2, 12-17; Psalm 51:1-17; 2 Corinthians 5:20b–6:10;
Matthew 6:1-6, 16-21

Theme Ideas

Ash Wednesday begins the forty-day journey of Lent—a
journey where we follow Jesus' steps to Jerusalem and,
ultimately, the cross. Ash Wednesday invites us to take
this journey of introspection and to reflect upon what it
means to be a Christian, what it means to take up one's
cross and to follow Jesus. The imposition of ashes on
our foreheads reminds us of the frailty of our lives here
on earth. We were created out of the dust of the earth,
and to dust we shall return. Divine judgment is at hand,
but this judgment is tempered with mercy and a call to
begin our journey anew.

Invitation and Gathering

Centering Words (Joel 2, Ps 51)

Storm clouds are on the horizon. The day of the Lord is at hand—a day of dread and despair. Yet even now, there is a chance of escaping the funeral shrouds we have woven for ourselves. There is a chance to start again.

Call to Worship (Joel 2, Ps 51)

Blow the trumpet in Zion.
Sound the alarm on God's holy mountain!
The day of the Lord draws near—
a day of darkness and gloom.
Yet even now, who knows if God will relent,
and turn our calamity into joy.
Let us rend our hearts, not our clothing.
Let us return to the Lord,
who abounds in steadfast love.
Leave behind the ways that lead to death,
and return to God with all your heart!
Have mercy on us, O God,
and put a new and right spirit within us.

—Or—

Call to Worship (Joel 2:12)

"Return to me!"
Christ calls, and we hear.
"Return to me!"
Christ calls, and we listen.
"Return to me!"
Christ calls, and we respond.
"Return to me!"
Christ calls, and we turn...
toward life, toward love, toward God.

Opening Prayer (Joel 2, Ps 51)

    With open hearts, merciful God,
        we desire to live in your grace.
    Speak to us with wisdom and mercy,
        with patience and perseverance,
            that we may hear your call
            and mend our ways.
    As we embark on this Lenten journey,
        walk with us and teach us your love,
            that we might be signs of your grace.
    With joyous hope, we pray. Amen.

Proclamation and Response

Prayer of Confession (Ps 51)

    Holy One, wash away our guilt
        and cleanse us from our shortcomings,
            for we have transgressed against you
                and turned away from your paths.
    You desire truth in our inward being,
        yet we reject the wisdom you place in our hearts.
    Create in us a clean heart, O God,
        and put a new and right spirit within us.
    Do not cast us away from your presence,
        and do not take your Holy Spirit from us.
    Lead us anew in the paths of life,
        that we might return to you with all heart. Amen.

Words of Assurance (Joel 2:12-13)

    Hear the words of the prophet Joel: "Yet even now, says
    the LORD, / return to me with all your hearts, / with fast-
    ing, with weeping, and with sorrow; / tear your hearts /
    and not your clothing. / Return to the LORD your God, /

for [God] is merciful and compassionate, / very patient, full of faithful love, / and ready to forgive."

Passing the Peace of Christ (Joel 2)

Throw off the garments of death, and embrace the life God offers us this day when we live as God intends. Let us share this joy as we turn and pass the peace of Christ.

Response to the Word

Holy One, remind us this day
of the frailty of our lives here on earth.
May your word grow in our hearts,
that we might live each day to the fullest.
Help us face our mistakes, return to your ways,
and commit ourselves to follow your Son
on the journey ahead.

Call to Prayer (Matt 6)

The One who dwells in secret hears the prayers of our hearts and the yearning of our spirits. Let us enter into silent prayer as we seek the One who sees in secret and rewards those who draw near.

Thanksgiving and Communion

Thanksgiving over the Ashes

God of dust and ash,
you fashioned us from the dust of the earth,
and to dust we shall return.
May the ashes from last year's palms
that we place on our foreheads this day
remind us of who we are
and whose we are.

Draw us back to you, O God,
>for you are gracious and merciful,
>>slow to anger, and abounding in steadfast love.
Heal the hardness of our hearts,
>that we may be faithful disciples
>>of the one who makes all things new. Amen.

Offering Prayer (Matt 6)
Gracious God, we have sought recognition for our piety,
>and taken pride in our giving.
Receive these offerings
>in the spirit of your Son,
>>who taught us to watch our hearts—
>>>for where our hearts are,
>>>>there our treasure will be also.
May our treasure be in you, Holy One,
>and in the welfare of our world. Amen.

Sending Forth

Benediction (Ps 51)
Wash us thoroughly from our iniquities,
and we will be whiter than snow.
>**Bathe us in your steadfast love.**
Create in us a clean heart, O God,
and help us hear the joy of your calling.
>**Restore to us the joy of your salvation.**
Go with God's blessing.

March 5, 2017

First Sunday in Lent

Mary J. Scifres

Color

Purple

Scripture Readings

Genesis 2:15-17; 3:1-7; Psalm 32; Romans 5:12-19; Matthew 4:1-11

Theme Ideas

While temptation is the most common theme that arises from today's readings, vulnerability also emerges as an important theme. Vulnerable first to the serpent's clever challenge, man and woman then stand vulnerable in the awareness of their nakedness before God. The vulnerability that arises from sinfulness emerges as a common theme in both Psalm 32 and Romans 5; and Jesus' vulnerability in the wilderness leads to temptation from the devil. Yet in our most vulnerable situations, God's grace and faithful love strengthen and sustain us, covering our vulnerability more abundantly than any fig leaves every could.

Invitation and Gathering

Centering Words (Gen 2–3, Luke 2)

Vulnerable and naked, we came into this world. Vulnerable and naked, God came to us on that long-ago Christmas morn. Let us come into God's presence, vulnerable and naked in spirit, knowing that we are safe and secure here.

Call to Worship (Matt 4)

In the wilderness of life, we are not alone.

God is with us, even in the midst of our loneliness.

On the treacherous paths, God's guidance is ours.

We will walk in God's ways of wisdom and truth.

Come to hear. Come to learn.

Come to the hiding place of God.

Here we find grace. Here we find love.

Here we will worship and pray.

Opening Prayer (Matt 4)

Faithful God, strengthen us for the journey ahead.

Guide us with your knowledge and your love.

Send your Spirit to drive us and guide us

where we need to go—

ever-closer to you and to your ways.

Proclamation and Response

Prayer of Confession (Gen 2-3, Ps 32)

God of mercy and grace,

cover our nakedness,

and strengthen our vulnerabilities.

Forgive us in our sinfulness,
    and surround us with your faithful love,
        that we may know true happiness
           through your mercy and grace.

Words of Assurance (Ps 32, Rom 5)

Faithful love surrounds you.
Forgiveness is yours, through the grace of Christ.
Rejoice and be glad!

Passing the Peace of Christ (Ps 32)

As we have been loved faithfully, let us share this love
with one another!

Introduction to the Word (Ps 32:8)

"I will instruct you and teach you / about the direction
you should go." These are the promises of God for the
people of God. Listen, wait, pray, think, and discover
where God leads.

Response to the Word (Matt 4)

(You may invite participants to pray silently after each invitation.)
In this season of forty days and nights,
    we are invited to wait with God.
In this season of forty days of Lent,
    we are invited to wander with God.
In this season of forty days before Easter,
    we are invited to walk with God.
Wait, even in the darkness.
Wander, even in the wilderness.
Walk, even on uncharted paths.
Together we will journey with God.

Thanksgiving and Communion

Offering Prayer (Matt 4)
Although we do not live by bread alone,
we do need food to sustain us.
Although we do not yearn for injury and illness,
they do come our way,
and we do need healing.
Bless these gifts to be sustenance and healing
for those in need.
Bless us to be sustenance and healing
for your world.
In Christ's name, we pray. Amen.

Invitation to Communion (Ps 32, Rom 5)
Are you hungry for God?
Come to the bread of life.
Are you in need of forgiveness?
Come to the table of grace.
Are you empty and alone?
Come to the feast of love.
Come, even when naked and vulnerable,
for here we are covered with abundant grace
and filled with the goodness of God.

Sending Forth

Benediction (Matt 4)
Even as we go forth on this journey,
God goes with us to guide our way.
Let us go forth with grace and love!

March 12, 2017

Second Sunday in Lent
Joanne Carlson Brown

Color

Purple

Scripture Readings

Genesis 12:1-4a; Psalm 121; Romans 4:1-5, 13-17; John 3:1-17

Theme Ideas

God is with us no matter what—when we are called to go where we do not know, when we are troubled and searching, when we have assurance of faith, when we experience Jesus in and with us. All these things are blessings from God—the doubt, the searching, the yearning, and the faith we come to. What a reassuring conviction that no matter where we are, or where we find ourselves on our spiritual journeys, there is God welcoming and walking with us.

Invitation and Gathering

Centering Words (Gen 12)
We are blessed to be a blessing.

Call to Worship (Gen 12, Ps 121, Rom 4)
We are called to go to places that we don't know.
We look to the hills for our strength.
Our strength is in God, who always goes with us.
We walk in faith.
Come, let us worship the God who calls us
and who walks beside us throughout the journey.

Opening Prayer (Gen 12, Ps 121, Rom 4, John 3)
Our ever-present strength and help,
we come this morning
in response to a call we have felt
in the marrow of our bones.
We may not be sure; we may even be full of doubts
and not fully understand how we got here,
but we are here.
Help us listen with new ears and open hearts.
Touch us during this time of worship,
that we may know your unconditional love—
not just for the world as a whole
but for us individually.
It is for this that we long
and for which we search. Amen.

Proclamation and Response

Prayer of Confession (Gen 12, Ps 121, Rom 4, John 3)
Loving and ever-present God,
we confess that we are not always sure of you.
Our doubts overwhelm us at times.
But we continue to search
and to yearn for reassurance
of your presence with us,
no matter what is going on in our lives.

In times of joy and in times of sorrows and challenges,
help us feel your presence with us.
Give us a faith that looks to the hills,
where we will find you, steadfast and sure.
Be with us on our journey,
the journey to which you call us,
that we may walk in your ways
with you beside us. Amen.

Words of Assurance (Gen 12, Ps 121, John 3)
God so loved the world—God so loved us—
that God goes with us every step of the way.
In this we are blessed.
Know that God hears, answers, and loves us—
and in this loving, understands and forgives us.

Response to the Word (Gen 12, Ps 121, Rom 4, John 3)
For the openness to hear your word;
for the faith that grows
in our hearts and minds;
for the strength to be on the journey together,
we give you thanks and praise.

Thanksgiving and Communion

Offering Prayer (Gen 12)
We have been blessed to be a blessing to the world.
May the gifts we dedicate and offer you this day,
bless a world in need,
not only with our material resources,
but with our very selves. Amen.

Sending Forth

Benediction (Gen 12, Ps 121, Rom 4)
Go now in the sure knowledge that God goes with you
every step of your journey.
Go to be a blessing to everyone you meet.
Go, surrounded by the steadfast
and strengthening love of God.
Go in faith to love and to serve God's people
wherever you go. Amen.

March 19, 2017

Third Sunday in Lent

B. J. Beu

Color

Purple

Scripture Readings

Exodus 17:1-7; Psalm 95; Romans 5:1-11; John 4:5-42

Theme Ideas

Without water to drink, the people perish. Without the waters of faith, our spirits wither and die. The good news is that God offers us both, and therein lies our hope. In Exodus, the Hebrews cried out to God and received water from a rock. In John, a woman at the well met Jesus and was offered waters that well up to eternal life. The psalmist entreats us to give thanks to the One who is the source of our hope and salvation. And Romans reminds us that God's love has been poured into our hearts through the power of the Holy Spirit. These scriptures remind us just who it is that quenches our thirst.

Invitation and Gathering

Centering Words (Exod 17, Rom 5, John 4)

Water gushing from a rock...Living waters welling up
to eternal life...These are gifts from the One who pours
love into our hearts, through the power of the Holy
Spirit. Come and drink deeply. Taste and see that our
God is good.

Call to Worship (Ps 95)

Come into God's presence with thanksgiving.
Worship the Holy One
with joy and thanksgiving.
Let us sing to our God.
Make a joyful noise
to the rock of our salvation.
For we are the sheep of God's pasture.
We are the lambs of God's flock.
Come into God's presence with thanksgiving.
Worship the Holy One
with joy and thanksgiving.

Opening Prayer (Exod 17, Rom 5, John 4)

Living water, flow through our hearts this day.
Meet us in our desert wanderings
and quench our thirst,
that we may have strength
for the hard times ahead.
Well up within us,
and bathe us in the waters of eternal life,
that the spirit within us
may flow with faith and love,
through the power of your Spirit. Amen.

Proclamation and Response

Prayer of Confession (Exod 17)
> Wellspring of salvation,
>> when we are parched from thirst
>>> and turn to the dry wells of worldly promise,
>>>> restore us with the healing waters
>>>>> of your grace;
>> when the course ahead is littered
>>> with wreckage and refuse from our past,
>>>> wash away our sins and our sorrows,
>>>>> and carry us forward on the river
>>>>>> of your mercy and your love.
> Shower us with your living water,
>> and refresh our souls,
>>> that we may be washed clean in the river
>>>> of your forgiveness and your grace. Amen.

Words of Assurance (John 4)
> Jesus said, "Ask, and I will give you living water.
>> Those who drink of this water will never be thirsty,
>>> for they will have a spring of water
>>> gushing up to eternal life."
> Ask, and you will receive.
> Seek, and you will find.

—Or—

Words of Assurance (Exod 17, Rom 5, John 4)
> Our hope and assurance rest in God's
>> unfailing love and forgiveness.
> In this love and forgiveness,
>> we encounter the living God.

Passing the Peace (Rom 5)

God is here, pouring love into our hearts through the power of the Holy Spirit. Let us open our hearts and minds to receive this love, as we share the peace of Christ with one another.

Introduction to the Word (Exod 17, John 4)

Listen, all who are thirsty!
Christ offers us living water.
Listen, all who feel too tired to carry on.
Christ offers us living water.
Listen, all who need the healing of God's Spirit.
Christ offers us living water.
Listen, and let the waters of life
wash over you and bless you.

Response to the Word (Rom 5, John 4)

Spring of eternal life, well up within us
and wash away our fears.
Sweep away the impediments
that keep our hearts from loving others
as you have loved us.
Give us the confidence of the Samaritan woman,
that we might share with others
the good news of your mercy and compassion.
In the promise of your grace, we pray. Amen.

Thanksgiving and Communion

Invitation to Offering (Rom 5, John 4)

Called to live in hope, let us share the blessings we have so richly received from God.

Offering Prayer (Exod 17, John 4)
  Eternal Spirit, Source of healing and wholeness,
    bless these gifts,
      that they may be Christ's promise
        of living water for the world.
  May all who are touched by today's offering
    be bathed in the goodness
      of God's life, grace and hope. Amen.

Sending Forth

Benediction (Exod 17, Rom 5, John 4)
  Bathe in the river of God's love.
  Swim in the waters of Christ's baptism.
  Ride the currents of the Holy Spirit.
  Share God's living water with a thirsty world
    and feel the blessings of God well up within you
    into a spring of eternal life.
  Go with God.

March 26, 2017

Fourth Sunday in Lent
Deborah Sokolove

Color

Purple

Scripture Readings

1 Samuel 16:1-13; Psalm 23; Ephesians 5:8-14; John 9:1-41

Theme Ideas

God looks past outward appearances, seeing the essence of who we are and leading us out of the shadows of fear and pain. Arrogance blinds us to our own sins, but magnifies the sins of others in our eyes. When we allow the light of God to shine in our hearts, we perceive God's comforting presence, even in our enemies. We are anointed to be channels of God's grace.

Invitation and Gathering

Centering Words (Ps 23, Eph 5, John 9)
Holy One, open our hearts to your comforting presence, that we may bear your light into the world.

Call to Worship (Ps 23, Eph 5, John 9)
The Holy One shows us the way,
even when we do not know where to go.
We are called to live as children of light,
abiding in all that is good and right and true.
The Holy One leads us in pleasant places,
filling our hearts with the waters of life.
We are called to follow Jesus,
bringing Christ's light into the shadows.
The Holy One shows us the paths of peace,
comforting us in times of trouble.
We are called to become the body of Christ,
pouring out our lives for the healing of the world.

Opening Prayer (1 Sam 16, Ps 23, John 9)
Maker of Visions, Spirit of Truth, Light of the World,
you choose the least and the weak
to be bearers of your good news.
Rejecting those who brag of their own triumphs,
you anointed your servant David to lead Israel,
when all he had ever done
was keep his father's sheep.
As we walk the uncertain paths before us,
anoint us with gladness and bless us with vision.
Show us the way through terror and shadow.
Fill us with your light,
that we may more fully be the body of Christ,
bringing light to an aching, broken world. **Amen**.

Proclamation and Response

Prayer of Confession (Ps 23, Eph 5, John 9)
Light of the World, Maker of Visions, Spirit of Truth,
you have called us to be light for the world.

We hide in the shadows,
    afraid to let anyone see us
        as we really are.
You call us to see the pain of others,
    to comfort the suffering
        and to be channels of your love.
Yet we close our eyes to the misery around us,
    afraid to change the way things
        have always been done.
You call us to show your beauty and truth,
    in all that we say and in all that we do.
Forgive us, Holy One, when we refuse to see
    the gifts you spread before us
        for the healing of your world.

Words of Assurance (Ps 23)
    The One who is the Light of the World restores us,
        guiding us onto right paths
        and filling us with light.
    In the name of Christ, we are forgiven, healed,
        and comforted.
    Our cups overflow with God's loving mercy.
    Thanks be to God. Amen

Passing the Peace of Christ (Eph 5)
    Filled with the light of forgiveness, let us greet one another with signs of peace.
    The peace of Christ be with you.
    The peace of Christ be with you always.

Prayer of Preparation (Ps 23)
    Holy One, open our hearts to your Holy Word.
    Help us hear your voice in the words we hear
    and in the silence that lies between them. Amen.

Response to the Word (1 Sam 16, John 9)
>Spirit of Truth, Light of the World, Maker of Visions,
>>we give you thanks for ancient stories
>>>made new today.
>>**As you guided Samuel to anoint David**
>>>**to be king of ancient Israel,**
>>>>**guide us to be worthy bearers**
>>>>>**of your wondrous light.**
>>**As you opened the eyes of the man born blind,**
>>>**open our eyes to your truth and beauty. Amen.**

Thanksgiving and Communion

Offering Prayer (Ps 23)
>Light of the World, our cup overflows
>>with gratitude for all that you have given us.
>Accept the tokens we offer you today
>>and use them for the healing of the world. **Amen**.

Great Thanksgiving
>Christ be with you.
>>**And also with you.**
>Lift up your hearts.
>>**We lift them up to God.**
>Let us give our thanks to the Holy One.
>>**It is right to give our thanks and praise.**
>It is a right, good, and a joyful thing,
>>always and everywhere, to give our thanks to you,
>>who fills our hearts with gladness,
>>and floods the earth with light.
>We give thanks for meadows and forests,
>>for formal feasts and picnics on the lawn,
>>for clean water that flows from taps

and falls from the sky
into rivers and streams and oceans.
We give thanks for prophets and seers,
for old stories and new songs,
for bread and wine and miracles of sight.
And so, with your creatures on earth
and all the heavenly chorus, we praise your name
and join their unending hymn, saying:
Holy, holy, holy Lord, God of power and might,
heaven and earth are full of your glory.
Hosanna in the highest. Blessed is the one
who comes in the name of the Lord.
Hosanna in the highest.
Holy are you, and holy is your child, Jesus Christ,
who gives sight to the blind
and fills our hearts with light.
On the night in which he gave himself up,
Jesus took bread, gave thanks to you,
broke the bread, and gave it to the disciples, saying:
"Take, eat; this is my body, which is given for you.
Do this in remembrance of me."
When the supper was over, Jesus took the cup,
offered thanks and gave it to the disciples, saying:
"Drink from this, all of you;
this is my life in the new covenant,
poured out for you and for many,
for the forgiveness of sins.
Do this, as often as you drink it,
in remembrance of me."
And so, in remembrance of your mighty acts
in Jesus Christ, we proclaim the mystery of faith.
Christ has died.

Christ is risen.
Christ will come again.
Pour out your Holy Spirit on us,
    and on these gifts of bread and wine.
Make them be for us the body and blood of Christ,
    that we may be the body of Christ
    to a world filled with temptation.
God of light and vision, God of mystery and truth,
    God of love and grace,
        we praise your saving, gracious name. **Amen.**

Sending Forth

Benediction (Ps 23, Eph 5)
Open your eyes and your heart to the light of God,
    even in the presence of your enemies.
For the vision of God's light
    is found in what is good and right and true.
Go forth as children of the light,
    in the name of the One who is Maker of Visions,
    Spirit of Truth, Light of the World. **Amen.**

April 2, 2017

Fifth Sunday in Lent

Mary J. Scifres

Color

Purple

Scripture Readings

Ezekiel 37:1-14; Psalm 130; Romans 8:6-11; John 11:1-45

Theme Ideas

Resurrection and the promise of new life surprise us in this season of Lent, but these themes emerge out of the dry dust of death, reminding us of resurrection's connection to the ashes of death and decay. Resurrection is a miracle only when we remember that we are mortal—ashes to ashes, dust to dust. Dry bones coming to life? A dead man walking forth from his tomb? These are surprising, shocking stories of God's mighty power—illustrations of Christ's miraculous promises. In a world full of aging churches and crumbling institutions, these scriptures provoke us with the possibility that the dry bones of our world may yet live. Come, Holy Spirit, come!

Invitation and Gathering

Centering Words (Ezek 34, John 11)

In the midst of life, we are in death. But in the face of death, God's Spirit comes to bring us life. Can dry bones live? Can life emerge from death? Only God knows. And yet, Christ promises just such a miracle through the power of God's Holy Spirit. Come, Holy Spirit, come.

Call to Worship (Rom 8, John 11)

All who are dwindling and dying...
   come forth to new life.
All who are lying in darkness and despair...
   come out into the light.
All who feel separated and alone...
   come to the presence of God,
   whose Spirit finds us here.

Opening Prayer (Rom 8, John 11)

Come, Holy Spirit.
Breathe new life into our lives
   and our worship.
Create new possibilities,
   in our imaginations and in our dreams.
Send the promise of your hope
   into our depression and our despair.
Expand our hearts and our minds,
   as we enter your presence this day.

Proclamation and Response

Prayer of Confession (John 11)

God of new life and emerging possibilities,

> forgive us when death and despair
>> occupy our focus.
> Embolden our faith
>> when your future feels out of reach.
> Strengthen our courage,
>> that we might come forth
>>> into the light and life of your promises.
> In hope and trust, we pray. Amen.

Words of Assurance (Ps 130, Rom 8)

> In God's love, there is hope.
> In Christ's forgiveness, there is peace.
> In the Spirit's power, we are renewed
>> and brought forth into life!

Passing the Peace of Christ (John 11)

> Come out of your seats to share signs of new life and hope. Join one another in sharing signs of Christ's peace.

Introduction to the Word (Ps 130, Rom 8)

> Let your ears be attentive.
> Let your minds be focused upon the Spirit.
> Listen for the word of God.

Response to the Word (Ezek 37)

> *(Encourage increasing excitement with each response.)*
> Friends, can these bones live?
>> **Only God knows.**
> Friends, can these bones live?
>> **God only knows!**
> Friends, can these bones live?
>> **God knows!**
> Friends, can we live?
>> **God promises we can!**

Thanksgiving and Communion

Invitation to the Offering (Rom 8)

Let us bring gifts of the Spirit, as we offer hope and life
to the world today.

Offering Prayer (Ezek 37)

With these gifts, mighty God, bring forth new life
and renewed hope.
Work in us and through,
that our lives and our gifts
may become signs of life and hope
for all to see.

Great Thanksgiving (Ezek 37)

Christ be with you.
And also with you.
Lift up your hearts.
We lift them up to God.
Let us give our thanks to the Holy One.
It is right to give our thanks and praise.
It is a right, good, and a joyful thing,
always and everywhere, to give our thanks to you,
Creator God, Maker of all that is,
and all that ever will be.
In ancient days, you created us from the dust of the earth
and inspired us up to be your people—
a people of life and hope.
When we turned away and saw only death and despair,
you remained steadfast and you blessed us.
You reclaimed and renewed us,
bringing forth new life and hope
through the power and presence of your Spirit.

In the fullness of time, you sent your Son, Jesus Christ,
　　to show us the path to new life
　　and the glorious promise of your resurrection.
And so, with your people on earth,
　　and all the company of heaven,
　　we praise your name
　　and join their unending hymn, saying:
　　Holy, holy, holy Lord, God of power and might,
　　　heaven and earth are full of your glory.
　　Hosanna in the highest. Blessed is the one
　　　who comes in the name of the Lord.
　　Hosanna in the highest.
Holy are you, and holy is your child, Jesus Christ,
　　who lived and died, and overcame death,
　　to show us the truth of eternal life,
　　through your eternal love.
On the night he faced down death,
　　Jesus took bread, gave thanks to you,
　　broke the bread, and gave it to the disciples, saying:
　　"Take, eat; this is my body given for you.
　　Do this in remembrance of me."
When the supper was over, Jesus took the cup,
　　offered thanks and gave it to his disciples, saying:
　　"Drink from this, all of you;
　　this is new life, my life in the new covenant,
　　poured out for you and for many,
　　for the forgiveness of sins.
　　Do this, as often as you drink it,
　　in remembrance of me."
And so, in remembrance of your mighty acts
　　and your promise of new life in Christ Jesus,
　　we proclaim the mystery of faith.

Christ has died.
Christ is risen.
Christ will come again.
Pour out your Holy Spirit on us,
and on these gifts of bread and wine.
Make them be for us the life and love of Christ,
that we may be the body of Christ,
made new with him,
through the power of your Holy Spirit,
and that we may be made one with you,
and one in ministry to all the world.
Through the Risen Christ,
with the Holy Spirit in your holy Church,
all honor and glory is yours, eternal God,
now and forevermore. Amen.

Sending Forth

Benediction (John 11)
Let those who were languishing and dying
rejoice.
We go forth with the promise of life.
Let those who have lain in the shadows of despair
take heart.
We go forth with the promise of light.
Let those who have known the separation of loneliness
feel union in life with the Spirit.
We go forth revived by the Spirit
to proclaim the glory of God.

April 9, 2017

Palm/Passion Sunday

Mary J. Scifres

Color

Purple

Palm Sunday Readings

Psalm 118:1-2, 19-29; Matthew 21:1-11

Passion Sunday Readings

Isaiah 50:4-9a; Psalm 31:9-16; Philippians 2:5-11; Matthew 26:14–27:66 (27:11-54)

Theme Ideas

The hour is at hand. The time has come. Jesus makes his final entry into Jerusalem, only to be betrayed, tried, and crucified a few days later. This is a day to remember and reflect on the culmination of Jesus' journey and the shocking reality his followers faced when they saw him convicted and killed. The hour is at hand. The time has come.

Invitation and Gathering

Centering Words (Matt 21, 26–27)

Hosanna, Christ enters our lives! Blessings are here. Yet haunting truths lurk in the shadows: Jesus does not survive the Jerusalem pilgrimage. Death comes even to the most innocent and loving of humanity. Celebration and sorrow intermingle in our world.

Call to Worship (Matt 21)

With palm branches and joy, we shout:
"Hosanna to Christ our Lord!"
With blessings and songs we come:
to worship and to praise.
With humility and love,
Christ comes to meet us now.

Opening Prayer (Isa 50, Phil 2)

Awaken our ears, O God.
Open our minds,
that we might recognize your voice
and discover your wisdom.
Guide our thoughts,
that we might adopt Christ's attitude
of humility and love.
Strengthen our resolve,
that we might walk with you to the end,
even if it means death on a cross.
In your holy name, we pray. Amen.

Proclamation and Response

Prayer of Confession (Matt 21, Matt 26)
>For the times we have mocked rather than blessed,
>>**forgive us.**
>For the moments we deny you and others,
>>**reclaim us.**
>For the times we have forsaken bonds of friendship,
>>**renew us.**
>When we are the ones being mistreated,
>>**bless us.**
>When we are the ones being denied and betrayed,
>>**love us.**
>Strengthen us to face the time of trial, O God,
>>**that we may remain faithful to you,**
>>>**faithful to one another,**
>>>>**and faithful to your gospel of love.**
>In hope and humility, we pray.
>Amen.

Words of Assurance (Ps 118)
>Give thanks to God, for God's faithful love
>>lasts forever!
>In this faithful love, we are forgiven
>>and strengthened in Christ.

Prayer of Preparation
>Holy One, as we center ourselves in worship:
>>help us recognize your presence in our midst;
>>help us hear your wisdom in the words of scripture
>>>and the message;
>>help us know your ways and remain faithful
>>>on this day, and in the days to come. Amen.

Response to the Word (Matt 26)

When we face the time of trial,
give us strength to remain faithful.
When the hour of sorrow comes,
give us strength to remain faithful.
When others fall away,
give us strength to remain faithful.
As we journey through Holy Week,
give us strength to remain faithful.

Thanksgiving and Communion

Call to the Offering (Matt 21)

Whether we are bringing a colt or spreading our clothes on the road, whether we are writing a check with many zeroes or dropping a few coins in the plate, our gifts are symbols of welcoming Christ. Every gift is a blessing. Every gift is needed. Let us welcome Christ as we share our offerings with God.

Offering Prayer (Matt 21)

Blessed are you, Christ Jesus,
as you come to us this day.
Blessed are you,
as you work through the gifts
we bring you now.
Blessed are you as you live in our lives,
helping us become faithful disciples
and stewards of your love.
Bless and strengthen our gifts,
that they may bless and strengthen others.
With gratitude and joy, we pray. Amen.

Sending Forth

Benediction (Matt 26)

> In the hours and days and week ahead,
> Christ goes with us, leading the way.
> **Where Christ leads, we will follow.**
> Let us journey together to the cross.
> **Where Christ leads, we will follow.**

April 13, 2017

Holy Thursday
B. J. Beu

Color

Purple

Scripture Readings

Exodus 12:1-4 (5-10) 11-14; Psalm 116:1-4, 12-19; 1 Corinthians 11:23-26; John 13:1-17, 31b-35

Theme Ideas

This service is a time of solemn reflection on Jesus' last night with his disciples. As we remember Christ's gift of love to us, we are invited to listen to scripture, share in Holy Communion and a foot-washing ceremony, and sing the songs of our faith. Jesus becomes a servant to his followers—the ones who betrayed him, denied him, and ran away in the face of danger. Jesus is an example of faithful living in an age of unfaithfulness. The foot-washing ceremony depicts the depth of Jesus' love for us and offers us a glimpse of true servanthood. How can we fail to live up to his example?

Invitation and Gathering

Centering Words (John 13)

The time of trial approaches. Betrayal and denial are near at hand. Our minds race ahead, yet the one we love calls us to be here now—grounded in love and transformed through service to others. They will know we are Christians by our love.

Call to Worship (Exod 12, Ps 116, 1 Cor 11, John 13)

This is a day of memory . . .
as we remember the saving love of God
and the claim Christ makes on our lives.
Gratitude calls us here.
This is a day of mystery . . .
as we eat of the bread of life
and drink from the cup of salvation.
Wonder invites us to go deeper.
This is a day of deep knowing . . .
as Christ washes our feet
and we feel the depth of God's love.
Love leads us home.

Opening Prayer (Exod 12, 1 Cor 11, John 13)

Gather us in your love, O God,
as Jesus gathered his disciples:
washing their feet,
and sharing his very self
in the Seder meal.
Gather us in your love, Eternal Spirit,
as we gather in Jesus' name:
washing one another's feet
and sharing Christ's gift of self
in the Lord's Supper.

Gather us in your love, Holy One,
>   that we may gather in you. Amen.

Proclamation and Response

Prayer of Confession (Adapted from Juliun of Norwich)
>   In our eyes, O God, we do not stand.
>   Our failings are ever before us,
>   and we feel crushed under their weight.
>   Yet in your eyes, Holy One, we do not fall,
>   for we are your beloved children
>   and shine with the glory of your image.
>   Help us accept the truth of both visions,
>   even as we acknowledge
>   that the deeper insight
>   belongs to you. Amen.

Words of Assurance (Exod 12, Ps 116)
>   In our suffering and distress,
>   God saves us from the snares of death
>   and offers us the cup of salvation.
>   All who call on the name of the Lord will be saved
>   and receive God's manifold blessings.

Passing the Peace (John 13)
>   Just as Christ has loved us, we too should love one another. Let us show who we are, and whose we are, as we share this love with one another. They will know we are Christians by our love.

Invitation to the Word
>   Listen for the word of God with your hearts opened wide. Listen for the wisdom of God with your minds

illumined by the Holy Spirit. Listen for the grace of God with the same humility as Christ when he washed the feet of his disciples. Listen.

Response to the Word (Ps 116, John 13)

May the words of scripture become for us
the living word of God:
as our hearts are opened,
our minds are enlightened,
and our spirits are blessed
with the humility of a servant.

Thanksgiving and Communion

Invitation to the Offering (Ps 116)

Let us return to the Lord the many blessings that we have received. Let us pay our vows to the Lord in the presence of God's people.

Offering Prayer (Ps 116, John 13)

Source of love and compassion,
fill us with a deep, spiritual longing
to taste the cup of your salvation
and to know the joys of servant ministry.
May the gifts we bring before you this day,
be a fulfillment of our vow
to offer you our very selves
and to be known by our love. Amen.

Invitation to Communion (Pss 34, 116, 1 Cor 11, John 13)

Our souls hunger for food that satisfies.
Taste and see that the Lord is good.
Our souls are dry and parched from thirst.

**Lift up the cup of salvation
and call on the name of the Lord.**
Our souls long for the bread of heaven.
Taste and see that the Lord is good.
Our souls yearn to drink of God' blessing.
**Lift up the cup of salvation
and call on the name of the Lord.**

Invitation to Foot Washing (John 13)
Loving Servant, when we imagine you
kneeling down to wash our feet,
the intimacy of your gift humbles us.
Tonight, as we come to have our feet washed,
give us the courage to enter the naked now
and experience the profound gift
of your presence in our lives.
As we embrace the life of a servant in your name,
help us comprehend the love that heals us,
the joy that completes us,
and the grace that sets us free. Amen.

Sending Forth

Benediction (Ps 116, John 13)
Blessed by God, we are called to live.
They will know we are Christians by our love.
Healed by Christ, we are called to love.
They will know we are Christians by our love.
Sustained by the Spirit, we are called to serve.
They will know we are Christians by our love.

April 14, 2017

Good Friday

B. J. Beu

Color

Black or None

Scripture Readings

Isaiah 52:13–53:12; Psalm 22; Hebrews 10:16-25; John 18:1–19:42

Theme Ideas

Suffering, rejection, and loss focus our readings. Although Isaiah 52 begins with the exaltation of God's servant, it is a chilling reminder of how easily we turn on God's chosen ones. Psalm 22, which Jesus quotes while hanging on the cross, conveys the sense of being abandoned by God when the forces of destruction hold sway. Peter's betrayal of his friend and teacher in the courtyard depicts how low we can sink, despite our love and convictions. *(Worship Note: If your congregation has a gold or brass cross on its Lord's Table, substitute a rough-hewn wooden cross with horseshoe nails at the place of Jesus' hands and feet.)*

Invitation and Gathering

Centering Words (John 18-19)

Like moths to the flame, we are drawn here this evening. We watch from the sidelines, afraid of what we
may see, and who may see us watching. We hear words
of denial and betrayal spoken just offstage, and we are
startled that the voices sound so familiar. We observe
Jesus being abandoned by the ones he loves. Like moths
to the flame, we are drawn here this evening.

Call to Worship (John 18–19)

The night is as silent as death.
   Gone are the loud hosannas
   sang by children in the streets.
The dishes remain unwashed in the upper room.
   The dregs from Jesus' cup have turned sour,
   the crumbs from Jesus' plate have grown stale.
Thirty pieces of silver buy the betrayal of a friend.
   Three questions in a courtyard shatter pledges
   of loyalty and love.
The cock crows; the whip cracks; the hammer falls.
   Heaven weeps as innocent blood is spilt.
The night is as silent as death.

Opening Prayer (Isa 52–53, Ps 22:1 NRSV)

Elusive One, suffering is a bottomless well.
Where do you go when all hope fades?
Where do you hide when grief and pain
   strip us of everything we hold dear?
We seek your presence and turn to you for rescue,
   only to bear the excruciating emptiness
      of your absence.

Your ways are beyond us, mysterious One,
     cloaking us like a funeral shroud.
Be with us when all lights go out
     and we stumble blindly in the dark.
Be with us, even when we deny and betray you. Amen.

Proclamation and Response

Prayer of Confession (Isa 53, Ps 22, John 18–19)
     Merciful One, we cannot get through this night alone.
     Help us remain faithful
          in the midst of our betrayals and denials.
     Help us stay awake during our times of trial,
          when our sweat flows like rivers of blood.
     Forgive us when we wash our hands of our culpability
          in the face of folly and evil.
     May we feel, in the marrow of our bones,
          the depth of our own frailty.
     Help us acknowledge the razor's edge
          that separates hope from despair
               in a world filled with so much pain. Amen.

Assurance of Pardon (Isa 52, Heb 10)
     Out of Christ's anguish,
          we shall see light.
     Out of Christ' suffering,
          we shall touch the mystery of love and grace
          that pours from the inexhaustible heart of God.

Passing the Peace of Christ (John 18)
     Judas betrayed Jesus with a kiss, a sign of peace. Let
     those of us who truly love Christ redeem that act of be-
     trayal by showing signs of genuine Christian love and
     peace on this holy night.

Introduction to the Word

Listen to a story of events that should never have transpired. Listen to moments of anguish that never should have been. Pray, with every fiber of your being, that the words read this night will change your hearts and lives forever. Listen for the word of God.

Response to the Word (Isa 52:15, 53:1)

Who are we in tonight's story? Are we Judas, who gave up on his friend and master? Are we Simon Peter, who yearned to remain faithful but was trapped by his fear? Are we rank and file disciples, who could not seem to stay awake when it was time to pray for strength? Are we Pilate, who washed his hands of hard choices? Are we the women, marginalized and dismissed, yet staying with him to the end? Who are we in tonight's story? (*A time of silence may follow.*)

Thanksgiving and Communion

Invitation to the Offering (Ps 22, John 18–19)

Let us pour ourselves out like water, that the gifts we offer the world this night may be worthy of the gift we have received from the one who poured out his life out for us.

Offering Prayer

God of infinite love and grace,
    no good deed goes unpunished.
So it was with the gift of your Son.
So it is with all who offer up their hearts
    in true freedom into the brokenness of your world.
Receive the gifts we bring this night.

Accept them and bless them,
>even when the world questions our motives
>and scoffs at our humble commitment
>to follow a crucified savior. Amen.

Sending Forth

Benediction
>(*This may be omitted on Good Friday.*)
>In the midst of our pain and anguish,
>>rage, rage against the dying of the light.
>
>Allow your suffering to take you
>>to that place where suffering is transformed
>>into love and life
>>in the very heart of darkness.
>
>(*Drape the cross with black cloth and extinguish the Christ candle. Have rubrics in the program for the people to depart in silence.*)

April 16, 2017

Easter Sunday
Deborah Sokolove

Color

White

Scripture Readings

Acts 10:34-43; Psalm 118:1-2, 14-24; Colossians 3:1-4; John 20:1-18

Theme Ideas

Despite appearances, death does not have the last word. The truth of God's love is revealed in the life, death, and resurrection of Jesus; in the life of the Church; and in our lives today.

Invitation and Gathering

Centering Words (Ps 118)
Christ is risen, and we live in him. Alleluia! Amen.

Call to Worship (Ps 118, Col 3, John 20)
Alleluia! Christ is risen.
Christ is risen, indeed!

Open the gates of justice and righteousness,
that we may give thanks to God.
  Today we enter the gates of the Holy One
  as the body of Christ.
We are called to do justice and love kindness.
  Today is the day of celebration and promise.
Alleluia! Christ is risen.
  Christ is risen, indeed!

Opening Prayer (John 20)
God of mystery, God of wonder and love,
    God of resurrection and new life;
      last night we wept,
        because we thought you were dead.
This morning, like Mary in the garden,
    we mistake you for someone else,
      and ask where you have gone.
But you have wakened us with sunshine,
    opening our eyes to daffodils and cherry blossoms,
    filling our ears with birdsong,
    filling our hearts with joy.
For you are not dead, but risen,
    and live among us now.
Christ is risen.
Christ is risen, indeed!
Alleluia! Amen.

Proclamation and Response

Prayer of Confession (Acts 10, Col 3)
God of life and love, we rejoice in our own salvation,
    but find it hard to forgive those
      who have hurt us.

You call us to seek the paths of peace and blessing,
    to be your face to everyone we meet,
        but it is easier sticking to well-traveled streets
        of anger and resentment.
We yearn to live in ease in heaven,
    but too often make life hard for people around us.
You call us to spread your word of resurrection,
    to witness to your love and grace for the world,
        but our lips remain silent.
Forgive us, Holy One,
    when we hold on to what we have,
        rather than share your gifts with the world.

Words of Assurance (Acts 10, John 20)
The One whom the prophets foretold,
    and of whom the Gospels testify,
        lives among us today.
In the love of the Creator;
    in the life, death, and resurrection of Christ;
        and in the power of the Holy Spirit,
        we are forgiven.
Alleluia! Amen.

Passing the Peace of Christ (Col 3)
Rejoicing in Christ's life among us,
let us share signs of peace.
The peace of Christ be with you.
The peace of Christ be with you always.

Response to the Word (John 20)
God of wonder and mystery, we give you thanks
    for the life, death, and resurrection of Jesus Christ,
        that has been made known to us
        in the words of scripture
        and in our lives today.

Like Mary, standing astonished in the garden,
    we do not always recognize your presence with us.
But when we hear your voice, we can truly say:
    "We have seen the Holy One,
        and we know that Christ is risen."
Alleluia! Amen.

Thanksgiving and Communion

Invitation to the Offering (Col 3)
    In gratitude for the gift of new life in Christ, let us bring
our gifts and our offerings this day.

Offering Prayer (Col 3)
    God of love and grace,
        for the love and life
            that you give us in Christ,
                we offer you these signs of our gratitude;
        for the compassion and mercy
            that you give us in the Holy Spirit,
                we offer you our thankfulness and praise.
    Receive these gifts in your holy name. Amen.

Great Thanksgiving
    Christ be with you.
        And also with you.
    Lift up your hearts.
        We lift them up to God.
    Let us give our thanks to the Holy One.
        It is right to give our thanks and praise.
    It is a right, good, and a joyful thing,
        always and everywhere, to give our thanks to you,
        who has raised Christ from the dead,

and who has given us the promise of new life
in his name.
We give you thanks for prophets and apostles,
for the disciples who ran to see the empty tomb,
for the faith and testimony of Mary Magdalene,
and for the women and men in every age
who have witnessed to the power of the risen Christ:
for healing, forgiveness, and new life.
And so, with your creatures on earth
and all the heavenly chorus, we praise your name
and join their unending hymn:
**Holy, holy, holy Lord, God of power and might,
heaven and earth are full of your glory.
Hosanna in the highest. Blessed is the one
who comes in the name of the Lord.
Hosanna in the highest.**
Holy are you, and holy is your son, Jesus Christ,
who in life brought healing and freedom
to all who were oppressed;
who even in death on the cross,
forgave his enemies;
and who rose from the dead and lives in us today.
On the night in which he gave himself up,
Jesus took bread, gave thanks to you,
broke the bread, and gave it to the disciples, saying:
"Take, eat; this is my body, which is given for you.
Do this in remembrance of me."
When the supper was over, Jesus took the cup,
offered thanks and gave it to the disciples, saying:
"Drink from this, all of you;
this is my life in the new covenant,
poured out for you and for many,
for the forgiveness of sins.

Do this, as often as you drink it,
in remembrance of me."
And so, in remembrance of your mighty acts
in Jesus Christ, we proclaim the mystery of faith.
Christ has died.
Christ is risen.
Christ will come again.
Pour out your Holy Spirit on us,
and on these gifts of bread and wine.
Make them be for us the body and blood of Christ,
that we may be the body of Christ
for all who yearn for new life.
God of newness and mystery,
God of wonder and love,
God of resurrection and new life;
we praise your name
and rejoice in our life in you. Amen.

Sending Forth

Benediction (John 20)
With Mary and the disciples
and all those who live in Christ,
let us rejoice that we have seen our Savior,
who is not dead, but lives.
In the love of the Creator;
in the life, death, and resurrection of Jesus Christ;
and the power of the Holy Spirit,
let us go forth to love and serve the world.
Christ is risen.
Christ is risen, indeed.
Alleluia! Amen.

April 23, 2017

Second Sunday of Easter
Mary Petrina Boyd

Color

White

Scripture Readings

Acts 2:14a, 22-32; Psalm 16; 1 Peter 1:3-9; John 20:19-31

Theme Ideas

Throughout these passages, we hear that God is with us, defeating death. Through Jesus Christ, God brings peace and life. As befits the Easter season, joy permeates these texts. Acts quotes Psalm 16, where one's whole being—heart, tongue, and body—rejoices with hope. First Peter speaks of the glorious joy that is beyond words. John 20 reflects a variety of emotions, offering the blessing of peace and the promise of life, as the disciples, including Thomas, realize that Jesus is risen.

Invitation and Gathering

Centering Words (John 20)

In the midst of doubt and confusion, when we don't know what to believe, Jesus comes with words of hope and comfort: "Peace be with you."

Call to Worship (Acts 2)
Know this:
Jesus was a man sent by God.
Listen carefully to these words:
God raised Jesus from the dead!
Know this:
We are witnesses to God's power.
Listen carefully to these words:
God frees us from death.
Come and worship the God who never abandons us.
We worship with hearts full of joy.
—*Or*—

Call to Worship (1 Pet 1)
We are born anew.
We have a living hope.
We have an enduring inheritance.
It is God's love for us.
We trust God.
We rejoice with hearts filled with praise.
Words cannot begin to express our joy.
How can we express what it means
to be invited into God's presence?
Let us worship God this day.

Opening Prayer (1 Pet 1, John 20)
Loving God, you are our refuge and our hope.
You instruct us in your truth
    and teach us the ways that lead to life.
Through your Son, Jesus,
    we inherit the abundance of your grace.
Even when the way is difficult,
    even when we struggle,

you are with us.
Speak your word of peace to our hearts,
    that we too may proclaim Jesus as Lord. Amen.

Proclamation and Response

Prayer of Confession (John 20, 1 Pet 1)
We haven't seen the truth.
We have only heard what others have said.
We worry that our doubts keep us from true belief.
We reject the rich inheritance you offer us
    as we pursue our own foolish ways.
Yet we long to know the truth
    and to understand you fully.
Come to us, bringer of peace.
Forgive our doubts; show us your ways,
    and lead us into your truth. Amen

Words of Assurance (Ps 16)
God is our refuge, protecting us, instructing us,
    and leading us on the way that leads to life.

Passing the Peace of Christ (John 2)
Again and again the risen Christ tells his disciples,
"Peace be with you." Christ still says to his followers,
"Peace be with you." Let us share this message with one
another today.

Prayer of Preparation (John 20, Ps 16)
God, we come to you as we are,
    with both our doubts and our faith.
Show us your path,
    as we reflect on your word.

Be present with us,
> that we may know your truth
>> and find life and joy in your ways.
Open our hearts and instruct our minds, O God,
> for you are our refuge and our hope. Amen.

Response to the Word (John 20, 1 Pet 1)
> Living Christ, you give us what we need
>> to transform our doubt into belief.
> You come, offering us peace,
>> and filling our lives
>>> with your living presence.
> With joy and rejoicing,
>> may we go forth, confident in your love.

Thanksgiving and Communion

Offering Prayer (Ps 16, John 20)
> You, O God, are our refuge.
> You provide for us
>> and keep us from stumbling.
> You offer us life itself
>> and the deep peace of your presence.
> We offer ourselves to you this day,
>> trusting in your grace.
> We affirm that you are our God.
> May these gifts honor you,
>> as they continue your work
>>> of offering the world a living hope.

Invitation to Communion (John 20)
> Thomas needed to encounter the living Christ in order
to believe. At the table today, Jesus is present, saying

"Peace be with you." Come to the table, where the one whose name is Love welcomes us, feeds us, and blesses us. Come and rejoice in God's blessings!

Sending Forth

Benediction (John 20)
You have heard the story.
You have seen new life in the risen Lord.
Christ is among us, now and forever.
Peace be with you.
Peace be with you always.

April 30, 2017

Third Sunday of Easter

B. J. Beu

Color

White

Scripture Readings

Acts 2:14a, 36-41; Psalm 116:1-4, 12-19; 1 Peter 1:17-23;
Luke 24:13-35

Theme Ideas

Luke's story of the walk to Emmaus carries so many
beautiful themes: Christ walks with us, even when we
are unaware of his presence; Christ stays with us when
we offer hospitality to strangers; Christ opens our eyes
to divine presence when we break bread together. Acts
invites us to respond to Christ's gifts by being baptized
with power of the Holy Spirit. The psalmist praises God
for rescue, promising faithful service in return. The epistle speaks of mutual love that is born in our hearts as we
respond to Christ. Christ meets us unrecognized, opens
our eyes, and offers us a glorious future. This is good
news indeed.

Invitation and Gathering

Centering Words (Luke 24)

Walking down the road of life, how often do we meet Christ in a stranger? Chances are good we won't recognize him, even though our hearts may burn within us. Chances are even better he will move on to bless another unless we offer hospitality to our fellow travelers. Walking down the road of life, look for Christ...and be prepared to find him in a stranger.

Call to Worship (Ps 116, 1 Pet 1, Luke 24)

When you feel alone, don't despair...
> **Christ is here.**

When your hope falters, open your ears...
> **God is still speaking words of comfort and love.**

When your spirit flags, open your hearts...
> **The Spirit is here to guide you home.**

Here in this house of worship...
enter, rejoice, and come home.

Opening Prayer (Luke 24)

God of mutual love,
> plant an imperishable seed of faith
> > within us this day.

Nurture the roots of life and hope within our souls,
> that our hearts might burn within us
> > when we hear your voice.

During times of suffering and doubt,
> help us grow strong and true,
> > through your enduring word.

Stay with us now and reveal your presence to us,
> as we show hospitality to strangers
> > and break bread in your name. Amen.

Proclamation and Response

Prayer of Confession (Luke 24)
God of Easter hope,
it is easy to dismiss your resurrection miracles
in the world we live in.
When we fail to recognize you on the road,
speak your enduring word to us,
that our hearts may yearn
to know you better.
Help us follow our hearts
when we meet you on the road
and invite you to stay with us,
that our eyes may be opened
your life-giving presence.
During times of confusion and doubt,
open our eyes to the many ways
you reveal yourself to us,
that we may have the confidence to
proclaim the miracle of Easter.

Words of Assurance (1 Pet 1)
In Christ Jesus, we find mutual love
and an imperishable seed of faith and joy.
Risen with Christ, we are born anew.

Passing the Peace of Christ (Luke 24)
There is a peace that comes only from welcoming Christ
in a fellow traveler on the journey of life. Turn to those
around you and offer these words of welcome and peace.

Invitation to the Word (Luke 24)
Risen Lord, open our ears this day,
that our hearts may burn within us
as we hear your resurrection story anew.

Response to the Word (Ps 116, 1 Pet 1)
>We will pay our vows to the Lord,
>>in the presence of God's people.
>We will pay our vows to the Lord,
>>as we purify our souls
>>>through obedience to God's enduring word.

Thanksgiving and Communion

Invitation to the Offering (Ps 116)
>What shall we return to the Lord for God's many gifts?
>What praise shall we sing to God for the blessings we
>have received? Let us pay our vows to the Lord in the
>presence of God's people.

Offering Prayer (Ps 116, Luke 24)
>Loving God, receive our thanks and praise.
>For your presence on the road,
>>we thank you.
>For opening your word to us,
>>we praise you.
>For revealing yourself to us
>>in the face of a stranger,
>>>we offer you our deepest gratitude.
>May the gifts of our hands
>>reveal the love in our hearts. Amen.

Communion Prayer (1 Pet 1, Luke 24)
>Come, O traveler unknown,
>>and walk with us on the road of life.
>Reveal to us your holy presence
>>in the breaking of the bread
>>>and the sharing of the cup.

Restore to us the fullness of life in your name,
   that we might be a people of mutual love,
      born of the imperishable seed
         of your love and grace. Amen.

Sending Forth

Benediction (1 Pet 1, Luke 24)
   As you meet strangers on the road,
   let mutual love increase.
      Born of the imperishable seed of God's love,
      we will grow in grace and power.
   As you experience Christ in the smile of another,
   be purified in the presence of the Holy One.
      Born to grow into oaks of righteousness,
      we go forth to reveal the glory of God in our lives.
   Go with God's blessings.

May 7, 2017

Fourth Sunday of Easter
Mary Sue Brookshire

Color

White

Scripture Readings

Acts 2:42-47; Psalm 23; 1 Peter 2:19-25; John 10:1-10

Theme Ideas

The Fourth Sunday of Easter is also known as Good Shepherd Sunday. Every year, the lectionary includes Psalm 23 and a reading from John 10, which describes Jesus both as the good shepherd and the gate through which the sheep are saved. Jesus promises that those who follow him will live life to the fullest, which is beautifully illustrated by Psalm 23. First Peter reminds us that Jesus is the shepherd who gathers in the sheep who stray.

Invitation and Gathering

Centering Words (Ps 23, John 10)

Sheep move slowly, chew on things repeatedly before digesting them, and stay close to one another. They remember the face and voice of their shepherd. God invites us to be like sheep: to chew on things, stay close together, and listen for the voice of our shepherd. God invites us into green pastures to know the love of our Good Shepherd.

Call to Worship (Ps 23)
Come in, all who are tired and thirsty.
The Good Shepherd leads us to grassy meadows and restful waters.
Come in, all who are anxious and afraid.
The Good Shepherd protects us and leads us through dark valleys.
Come in, all who are empty and exhausted.
The Good Shepherd fills our lives with goodness and faithful love.
Come in, to be refreshed, to rest, and to receive.
The Good Shepherd has brought us here.

Opening Prayer (Ps 23, John 10, 1 Pet 2)
God, Beloved Shepherd, Guardian of our souls,
we come to listen for your familiar voice.
Call to us above the noise of our lives.
Gather us in from our comings and goings.
Feed us in the pastures of your love
and lead us to abundant life. Amen.

Proclamation and Response

Prayer of Confession (Ps 23, John 10, 1 Pet 2)
Loving Shepherd, you lead us along right paths
and give us abundant life.
Still, we resist your call.

We want to be in control;
>   we wish to determine our own direction.
Forgive us when we ignore your voice and turn away.
Bring us back into your fold
>   through the gates of your redeeming love.

Words of Assurance (1 Pet 2)

Even when we stray like sheep,
>   the Good Shepherd finds us and brings us home.
Through Christ, we are forgiven.

Introduction to the Word (Ps 23 NRSV)

The Lord is my shepherd. I shall not want. God makes me lie down in green pastures and leads me beside still waters. The Good Shepherd restores my soul.

Response to the Word (Ps 23 NRSV)

Surely goodness and mercy shall follow me all the days of my life, and I shall dwell in the house of the Lord my whole life long.

Thanksgiving and Communion

Invitation to the Offering (Ps 23)

The Good Shepherd provides for our needs; we lack nothing. We come now to share from the abundance that we have received.

Offering Prayer (John 10)

Holy One, we offer these gifts with gratitude
>   for the many ways you care for us.
Use these gifts, and our very lives, O God,
>   that all might have life, and have it abundantly.
Amen.

Sending Forth

Benediction (Ps 23, John 10)
    As you go out into the world,
        practice being sheep... and slow down.
    Chew on things. Stay close together.
    And listen for the voice of the shepherd calling to you.
    Amen.

May 14, 2017

Fifth Sunday of Easter; Festival of the Christian Home/Mother's Day

Mary J. Scifres

[Copyright © 2016 by Mary J. Scifres. Used by permission.]

Color

White

Scripture Readings

Acts 7:55-60; Psalm 31:1-5, 15-16; 1 Peter 2:2-10; John 14:1-14

Theme Ideas

Christ is our strong foundation, the cornerstone of our spiritual household as we honor and serve God. Living into this calling is never easy, which is seen dramatically in the martyrdom of Stephen. And yet, Christ promises to be with us both now and into eternity, preparing us to serve on this earth, but also preparing a place for us in God's household when we come to the end of our earthly journey.

Invitation and Gathering

Centering Words (1 Pet 2, John 14)
Come to Christ, the living cornerstone. Come to rest on the foundation of God's love. Come to be strengthened and renewed in the power of God's Holy Spirit.

Call to Worship (Ps 31, 1 Pet 2)
Once we were not a people,
but now we are God's people.
Once we were alone,
but together we are the household of God.
Here in this time of worship,
and later when we go forth to serve,
Christ is our cornerstone,
strengthening us for the journey.
In our living and in our dying,
Christ is our sure foundation,
strengthening us along the way.

Opening Prayer (Ps 31, 1 Pet 2)
Shine your face upon us, O God.
Help us see your face in one another
and hear your voice in the words that are spoken.
Through your grace, make us holy,
that we may offer spiritual sacrifices
that honor and glorify your holy name. Amen.

Proclamation and Response

Prayer of Confession (Acts 7, Ps 31, 1 Pet 2)
Gracious God, prepare us for the difficult road ahead.
Like Stephen, help us be ready to forgive
even the most horrendous of sins.

Like the psalmist, help us accept
    your forgiveness and grace.
Like newborn infants, help us receive
    your unconditional love.
(A time of silent confession may follow.)
With steadfast love, shine your face upon us,
    that we may know the beauty
        of your mercy and your grace.
In Christ's beloved name, we pray. Amen.

Words of Assurance (1 Pet 2)
Whoever believes in Christ will never be shamed,
    for in Christ we are forgiven and loved.

Passing the Peace of Christ (Ps 31, 1 Pet 2)
Together as God's people, let us shine upon one another
with signs of grace and peace.

Words of Preparation (1 Pet 2)
Yearn for the pure milk of God's holy word, that God's
word may take root in your lives and grow into a strong
foundation of faith and love.

Response to the Word (1 Pet 2)
Creator God, build us together
    into your household of love,
        that we may be your people
            and a strong community of faith.
Establish us upon the foundation of Christ,
    who is our rock and our redeemer. Amen.

Thanksgiving and Communion

Invitation to the Offering (1 Pet 2)
> As the people of God, let us bring our offerings and gifts, so that others may know the loving foundation we have found in Christ Jesus.

Offering Prayer (Ps 31, 1 Pet 2)
> Through these gifts, proclaim your word of grace.
> Shine forth through our offerings and our lives,
>> that others may see your face
>>> and know your steadfast love.
> In your love and grace, we pray. Amen.

Sending Forth

Benediction (Acts 1, John 17)
> As we have been strengthened,
>> **we go forth to strengthen others.**
> As we have been blessed,
>> **we go forth to bless the world.**
> As we have been loved,
>> **we go forth to love with compassion and grace.**

May 21, 2017

Sixth Sunday of Easter

B. J. Beu

Color

White

Scripture Readings

Acts 17:22-31; Psalm 66:8-20; 1 Peter 3:13-22; John 14:15-21

Theme Ideas

Love and suffering seem to be the two great paths to God. Suffering gets our attention and is a great vehicle of transformation, while love shows us the nature of God. The psalmist speaks of being tested and tried as silver is tried. God put other nations over Israel in order to lead the Israelites through fire and water into a spacious place of blessing. The epistle speaks of the suffering that will come from following Christ, and then urges the people to do good works anyway. For it is better to suffer for doing good than for doing evil. In the Gospel reading, Jesus promises the disciples that he will not leave them comfortless, but will send them the Advocate, the Holy Spirit, to teach them the truth about God and holy love. The reading from Acts does not fit this theme, but recounts the story of Paul in the Areopagus, proclaiming the God of Jesus Christ as the one the Athenians worshiped as an unknown god. Acts and the epistle also share the theme of searching and groping for God and ultimate truth.

Invitation and Gathering

Centering Words (Ps 66, John 14)

Tried as silver is tried, we have come through the fire to a place of blessing and promise. The One who loves us has not left us orphaned, but sends the Holy Spirit to lead us onto the great path of love.

Gathering Words (Acts 17, John 14)

From fire and storm, we come, O God.
Gather us in, and make us whole.
From suffering and pain, we come, Holy One.
Gather us in, and make us one.
From the highways of life, we come, Great Spirit.
Gather us in, and make us your disciples.

Opening Prayer (Ps 66, 1 Pet 3, John 14)

Refiner's Fire, purify our lives like precious silver,
    that our hearts may glow with holy love
        and leave the suffering of the past behind.
Holy flame, burn away our fears and regrets,
    that our spirits may move boldly into your future
        and shine with the luster of burnished gold.
Forge of truth, mold us into vessels of compassion,
    that our lives may reveal your glory
        and abide in your gracious love. Amen.

Proclamation and Response

Prayer of Confession (1 Pet 3, John 14)
Eternal God, in our quest to fulfill our lives,
we have abandoned your commandment of love
and turned our backs on pursuing what is right;
we have sought our own comfort and ease,
and turned away from easing the plight of others.
Forgive our failure to find ourselves in you.
Nurture the hope that is in us—
hope nurtured by our life in Christ,
hope found in your commandment of love—
that we may live as your children
and abide in your Spirit. Amen.

Assurance of Pardon (Ps 66)
Even when we journey through fire and water,
and are tested like silver in the flame,
God sees us through to the other side
and brings us to a place of laughter and light.
The Advocate meets us in our suffering
and heals us in holy love.

Passing the Peace of Christ (Ps 66, John 14)
Having been put to the test through fire and water, come
and lay your burdens down. Rest in the sanctuary of
God's healing love. And when you are ready, share the
peace of Christ with one anther—the peace promised
through the Holy Spirit.

Introduction to the Word (Acts 17, Ps 66, John 14)
Search for God, seekers of the way.
Grope for truth, disciples of wisdom.

Where shall we go to find what we seek?
And where shall we look for answers?
Come to the fountain of grace.
Here, we find what we are looking for.

Response to the Word (1 Pet 3, John 14)
Spirit of truth, you have spoken and are speaking still.
Help us hear your voice
    and respond with our very lives.
May we live your commandment of love
    and abide in your Holy Spirit,
        that the paths we walk
            may reveal your presence to the world.
            Amen.

Thanksgiving and Communion

Invitation to the Offering
We who love God are led by the Helper and Advocate to
be more than hearers of the word, but doers of the word
as well. Let us open ourselves now to the joy of sharing
God's love and concern with the world.

Offering Prayer (Ps 66, 1 Tim 3)
Healing God, when we went astray,
    you purified us with fire
        and washed us clean
            in the waters of our baptism.
In gratitude and thanks
    for your constant care and your many blessings,
        we return these gifts to you now,
            that they may bring hope and light
                to a world in need. Amen.

Sending Forth

Benediction (Acts 17, John 14)
>Once we searched and groped for God in darkness.
>>**Now we reside with Christ in glorious light.**
>Once we worried that God was far from us.
>>**Now we rejoice that God is closer to us**
>>**than our very breath.**
>Once we yearned for God's love and acceptance.
>>**Now we dwell in communion with God**
>>**and with one another.**

May 28, 2017

Seventh Sunday of Easter

Mary J. Scifres

Color

White

Scripture Readings

Acts 1:6-14; Psalm 68:1-10, 32-35; 1 Peter 4:12-14; 5:6-11; John 17:1-11

Alternate Readings for Ascension Day

Acts 1:1-11; Psalm 47; Ephesians 1:15-23; Luke 24:44-53 *(See online supplemental materials for a complete Ascension Day entry.)*

Theme Ideas

The power of God's Holy Spirit brings many gifts to the disciples in the early days after Jesus' death: the strength to wait, the ability to be Christ's witnesses, the courage to endure, and the gifts to build Christ's church. John 17:11 provides the hope behind the Advocate's gifts: "that they will be one," as God's Holy Trinity is One.

Invitation and Gathering

Centering Words (Acts 1, John 17)
> Called to be one with Christ, called to be one with each other, called to be one in ministry, we gather in the unity of God's Holy Spirit, who calls us here.

Call to Worship (Acts 1, John 17)
> Called to be one,
> **we are here.**
> Called to be strong,
> **we are here.**
> Called in devotion to God,
> **we gather to worship and pray.**

Opening Prayer (Acts 1, John 17)
> Holy Spirit, descend upon us this day.
> Gather us into your presence,
> that we may be devoted to prayer
> and strengthened in unity and love.
> In your holy name, we pray. Amen.

Proclamation and Response

Prayer of Confession (Ps 68, John 17)
> Rouse us with your grace and mercy, O God.
> Scatter the fears within our hearts.
> Drive away our doubt and our sin.
> Melt our insecurities and anxieties.
> Banish our divisions and disagreements,
> that we may be one with you
> through the grace of Christ Jesus,
> and one with each other

through the power of your Holy Spirit,
in whose name we pray. Amen.

Words of Assurance (Ps 68, John 17)
Sing to God! For we are forgiven and united
by God's power and grace.

Passing the Peace of Christ (John 17)
Forgiven by Christ's grace and united in the Spirit, let us
share signs of unity and love this day.

Prayer of Preparation (Ps 68, John 17)
Protector of orphans, defender of widows,
come to our aid this day,
for we are your children.
Help us hear your fatherly advice
and trust your motherly support.
Reveal your presence to us
in the glory of your word this day.

Response to the Word (1 Pet 4–5, John 17)
Dear friends, don't be dismayed
when fiery trials come our way.
God's Spirit will help us endure.
Struggles are not strange.
Anxieties are not new.
God's Spirit will help us endure.
Divisions may arise.
Disagreements will come.
God's Spirit will make us one.
Disunity dogs our steps.
We may feel orphaned and alone.
**Yet God's Spirit gathers us together,
strengthens us for the journey,
and calls us into unity and love.**

Thanksgiving and Communion

Invitation to the Offering (Ps 68)
Showered with God's abundant grace, let us share abundant love in the gifts and offerings we bring.

Offering Prayer (Ps 68, John 17)
Pour out your Holy Spirit on us.
Pour out your Holy Spirit on these gifts.
And pour out your Holy Spirit on the ministries
    we offer to your world.
Though our gifts and our offerings,
    may others may find generous friends
        and a loving community of faith.

Sending Forth

Benediction (Acts 1, John 17)
Called to be one,
    we go forth in unity and love.
Called to be strong,
    we go forth in the power of the Holy Spirit.
Called in devotion to God,
    we go forth in ministry and witness to the world.

June 4, 2017

Pentecost Sunday

B. J. Beu

Color

Red

Scripture Readings

Acts 2:1-21; Psalm 104:24-34, 35b; 1 Corinthians
12:3b-13; John 7:37-39

Theme Ideas

As Jesus' disciples huddled together in fear, the Holy
Spirit entered their dwelling in rushing wind and
tongues of fire. In that moment, the Church was born.
Without Pentecost, the gospel would not have moved
beyond that group of disciples huddled in the upper
room. The Spirit that was promised to the prophet Joel is
active in our world today, granting visions and dreams
to our old and young alike. The power of God to create
and renew life is the power of the Holy Spirit. We see
this power in the psalmist's hymn of praise. We behold
this power in Paul's discussion of adoption in Christ
through the Spirit. And we see the promise of this power in Jesus, as he comforts his disciples before his death.

Invitation and Gathering

Centering Words (Acts 2)

Remember a time when your hopes and dreams died. Remember your feelings of despair and powerlessness. Then remember your surprise when something stirred within, when new seeds of hope sprouted forth. That is the power of the Holy Spirit, the power of Pentecost.

Call to Worship (Acts 2, Ps 104)

With rushing wind and holy fire...
Come, Holy Spirit, come.
With tongues of flame and hopes rekindled...
Come, Holy Spirit, come.
With visions birthed and dreams restored...
Come, Holy Spirit, come.
With spacious grace and depth untold...
Come, Holy Spirit, come.
With rushing wind and holy fire...
Come, Holy Spirit, come.

Opening Prayer (Acts 2, 1 Cor 12, John 7)

Spirit of Pentecost, blow open the doors
of our shut up hearts,
and set our tongues free
to proclaim your praise.
Bestow your gifts on all people,
that our youth may have visions,
our elders may dream dreams,
and our sons and daughters may prophesy.
Blow into our lives,
and renew us as a people of faith,
that we may find the strength and courage
to be the people you call us to be. Amen.

Proclamation and Response

Prayer of Confession (Acts 2, Ps 104, 1 Cor 12, John 7)
Spirit of wind and flame, you set us free
from prisons of our own making,
yet we cling to the fears that jail us.
Source of living water, you draw us to Christ,
that our hearts may overflow with living water,
yet we shun the intimacy of your invitation.
Come once more in rushing wind and cleansing fire,
that we may embrace your gifts
in service to a world in need. Amen.

Words of Assurance (Acts 2, Ps 104)
God sends forth the Holy Spirit
and the face of the earth is renewed.
God sends this same Spirit to us,
that we too may be renewed and made whole.
Rejoice, sisters and brothers,
God's steadfast love endures forever.

Passing the Peace of Christ (1 Cor 12)
Renewed with the gifts of the Spirit, and blessed by
visions and dreams of peace in our world, let us share
Christ's peace with one another.

Introduction to the Word (Acts 2, John 7)
Can a locked door keep the Holy Spirit from releasing us
from our fears? Can a quaking spirit keep us from receiving the Spirit's gifts today? Can the church be born again
after two thousand years of inertia and indifference? Does
the story of Pentecost have anything to say to us today?
Listen for the word of God—listen, that our hearts may
be kindled with holy fire and overflow with living water.

Response to the Word (1 Cor 12, John 7:38b)

Jesus proclaimed: "Out of [the believer's heart] will flow rivers of living water." With the gifts of the Holy Spirit, may our hearts overflow with living water on this day of Pentecost, and on every day of our lives.

Thanksgiving and Communion

Invitation to the Offering (Ps 104, 1 Cor 12)

We worship a God who is with us to the end. When God opens her hand, we are filled with good things. When God closes his hand, our bodies return to the dust, and our breath returns to God, who gave it. In the time that is given us, and with the gifts of the Holy Spirit, let us share the bounty that God has given us in the hope that all may come to know the bounty of our God.

Offering Prayer (Ps 104, 1 Cor 12, John 7)

For opening your hand,
    and blessing us with your manifold blessings,
        we give you thanks.
On this day of Pentecost,
    we leave the safety of our hideouts
        and open our hearts to our fellow creatures.
May these gifts bring dreams and visions
    to world in need of hope and direction.
May they refresh our community of faith,
    that as we turn to Christ in our need,
        our hearts may overflow
            with rivers of living water. Amen.

Sending Forth

Benediction (Acts 2, Ps 104)

With rushing wind and holy fire,
go forth in the power of the living God.
We go forth as God's children.
With tongues of flame and hope rekindled,
go forth in the power of the eternal Christ.
We go forth as heirs with Christ.
With visions birthed and dreams restored,
go forth in the power of the Holy Spirit.
We go forth as new creations in God's Spirit.
With spacious grace and depth untold,
go forth in the mystery of the Holy One.

June 11, 2017

Trinity Sunday

B. J. Beu

Color

White

Scripture Readings

Genesis 1:1–2:4a; Psalm 8; 2 Corinthians 13:11-13;
Matthew 28:16-20

Theme Ideas

Trinitarian theology shows that the nature of God is
relational and communal. In relationship we live and
move and have our being with God and with one another. But because the Christian Trinity is a fourth-century
construct, we should not expect these texts to illuminate
Trinitarian theology. We can, however, use Trinitarian
theology as a lens to view these texts. While the first creation story focuses on the goodness of creation, it begins
with God (v.1), Spirit (v.2) and word (v.3), and ends with
God creating human beings in God's ("Our") likeness.
The psalmist continues with the blessings of creation.
The letter to Corinth speaks of the grace of Christ, the

love of God, and the communion of the Holy Spirit. Finally, Matthew's Gospel issues Christ's great commission: to make disciples of all nations and to baptize in the name of the Father, Son, and Holy Spirit.

Invitation and Gathering

Centering Words (Gen 1, Ps 8)

Are we ready to call God our Mother or Father? Are we prepared to hear God say to us, "You are very good!"? Can we leave our doubts and insecurities behind and claim our heritage? Will we stand in our truth?

Call to Worship (Gen 1, Ps 8)

God, how majestic is your name in all the earth.
Your glory surrounds and enfolds us.
Your image resides within us and completes us.
You made us but a little lower than the angels.
How majestic is your name in all the earth.

Opening Prayer (Gen 1)

Triune God, your Spirit danced over the waters,
    your Word was spoken,
        and the glory of your creation sprang forth:
            sun and moon, earth and sky,
                creatures beyond count.
We thank and praise you
    for putting your image within us
        and for creating us but a little lower
            than the angels.
Abide in us, as you abide in the fullness
    of your holy mystery.
Teach us to be caretakers and stewards

of your good earth,
    that we may walk gently upon the meadows,
    and leave puddles of light
      wherever we tread. Amen.

Proclamation and Response

Prayer of Confession (Gen 1, Ps 8, 2 Cor 13)
    God of grace and glory,
      who are we that you are mindful of us?
    You sustain us through the gift
      of your indwelling Presence,
        yet we turn from you again and again,
          and succumb to feelings of inadequacy
          and despair.
    We turn from communion with you
      and with one another,
        even though it is only in community
          that we have the strength to endure
          the mystery of your glory
            and weight of our failings.
    Claim us anew as your beloved children,
      and we will be healed. Amen.

Words of Assurance (Ps 8)
    The love of God, the grace of Jesus Christ,
      and the blessings of the Holy Spirit
      are ours without price or condition.
    Rejoice in this good news and live.

Passing the Peace of Christ (2 Cor 13)
    Sisters and brothers, when we live in peace with one an-
    other, the peace and love of God are ours. Let us share

this great gift with one another as we share signs of the
peace of Christ.

Response to the Word (Gen 1, Ps 8, Matt 28)
In the beginning, God was.
In the beginning, the Spirit brooded.
In the beginning a Word was spoken.
The rest is history.
And it was good.
It was very good.

Thanksgiving and Communion

Invitation to the Offering (Gen 1, Matt 28)
God has made us stewards and caretakers of this amazing planet, giving us responsibility to care for one another. Let us show our gratitude by sharing the blessings we have received from God to the glory of God's
purposes.

Offering Prayer (Gen 1)
Your gifts overwhelm us, Creator God.
We praise you for placing your image within us—
    an image that makes us who we are.
May these gifts reflect the glory of your image
    as they go forth to move creation forward
        toward its fulfillment in you. Amen.

Sending Forth

Benediction (2 Cor 13)
Go forth in the fullness of holy mystery.
May the love of God enfold you.

May the grace of Christ Jesus flow through you.
And may the communion of the Holy Spirit
    complete you.

—*Or*—

Benediction (2 Cor 13)

Abide in God's blessings
    and make known the image of God
    that resides within you.

June 18, 2017

Second Sunday after Pentecost, Proper 6; Father's Day

Mary J. Scifres

Color

Green

Scripture Readings

Genesis 18:1-15; Psalm 116:1-2, 12-19; Romans 5:1-8; Matthew 9:35–10:8 (9-23)

Theme Ideas

With God, all things are possible. These hopeful words of Matthew 19:26 are reflected in all of today's readings. When Sarah laughs at the absurd idea of finally bearing a child in her old age, Abraham is reminded that for God, "nothing is too difficult" ("wonderful" in the NRSV). Just as miraculously, we are all saved by faith, not by works, and even humble disciples are empowered to cast out demons and cure all manner of illness. These are the miracles of God, providing a hope that passes all understanding.

Invitation and Gathering

Centering Words (Gen 18, Matt 10)
Hope in God. Expect miracles. For with God, anything is possible!

Call to Worship (Ps 116, Rom 5)
We call to the Lord,
and God hears our prayers.
We lift up our praise,
and God hears our songs.
We wait for the Lord,
and God answers our hope.

Opening Prayer (Gen 18, Matt 10)
Miraculous, wonderful One,
come to us now.
Pour out your grace and your love.
Shower us with the power of your Holy Spirit,
that we may become people of miracles—
people filled with the laughter of hope.

Proclamation and Response

Prayer of Confession (Gen 18)
Holy One, be with us in our weakness.
When we laugh out of fear,
calm us with your courage.
When we laugh out of doubt,
empower us with your faith.
When we laugh out of our confusion,
guide us with your wisdom.
Transform our nervous laughter

into songs of praise
and shouts of joy and trust.
In your blessed name, we pray. Amen.

Words of Assurance (Gen 18, Rom 5)
In God's faithfulness, we are made righteous.
In Christ's love, we find peace and hope.
In the Spirit's strength, our laughter of derision
is transformed into laughter of joy.
Thanks be to God!

Passing the Peace of Christ (Rom 5)
With Christ's peace in our hearts and God's hope in our
lives, let us share signs of joy and love this day.

Response to the Word (Gen 18, Rom 5)
God, when trouble is on our doorstep,
strengthen us with endurance.
When our endurance wears thin,
transform endurance into character.
When our character feels under siege,
let our character grow into hope.
When our hope is shattered and we find it hard to trust,
grant us hope that does not disappoint,
that we may laugh with faith and joy,
even in the face of seeming impossibilities.

Thanksgiving and Communion

Invitation to the Offering (Matt 9)
The size of the harvest is bigger than we ever imag-
ined. God needs each and every gift we have if we are
to bring in the harvest and transform the world with

healing, hope, and love. Come, let us join in the harvest
by sharing our gifts.

Offering Prayer (Gen 18, Rom 5, Matt 9)
Bless these gifts, O God, with your hope and love,
    that others may know your healing power
        and your miraculous possibilities.
In joyous trust, we pray. Amen.

Sending Forth

Benediction (Gen 18, Rom 5)
Go now in peace.
Laugh this week with hope.
Take God's love with you wherever you go!

—*Or*—

Benediction (Gen 18, Rom 5)
Go now in peace.
Go now in hope.
Go now with the love of God.

June 25, 2017

Third Sunday after Pentecost, Proper 7
Karin Ellis

Color

Green

Scripture Readings

Genesis 21:8-21; Psalm 86:1-10, 16-17; Romans 6:1b-11;
Matthew 10:24-39

Theme Ideas

These scriptures are hard to hear. In the Genesis passage,
Abraham is asked by his wife to "cast out" Hagar and
her son. And in the Matthew passage, we hear Jesus proclaim that he has not come to bring peace, but a sword
to sow conflict among family members. But through
these stories, and through the words of the psalmist and
of Paul, we realize that God provides for us, especially
in the midst of adversity. God brings healing and new
life. God proclaims, "Do not fear," and those who hear
and follow Christ find new life.

Invitation and Gathering

Centering Prayer (Gen 21, Matt 10)
Ever present God,
help us to focus our hearts
and our minds on you.

Awaken us to your words: "Do not fear."
Reassure us with your unconditional love
    and your promise of new life in Christ.

Call to Worship (Ps 86)

People of God, incline your ear
and listen to the word of God.
    We come with open hearts,
    ready to receive God's word
    of forgiveness and love.
Call on the One who abounds in steadfast love.
    We are ready to proclaim the good news of God
    in this place and throughout the earth!

Opening Prayer (Rom 6, Matt 10)

God of love and grace,
    we gather in thanksgiving and praise.
Reassure us once more,
    that you never leave us or forsake us.
Empower us by your Holy Spirit,
    that we may live faithfully as people of Christ.
Help us leave behind the things that weigh us down,
    that we may find new life in Christ. Amen.

Proclamation and Response

Prayer of Confession (Gen 21, Rom 6, Matt 10)

Compassionate God, we come before you
    with humble hearts.
There are times in our lives:
    when we stray from your ways;
    when we bring conflict to our loved ones;
    when we become lost in the desert
        as we flee from your presence;

when we allow fear to govern our decisions
    and our actions;
when we choose the ways of the world
    instead of the ways of Christ.
Forgive us, God of life.
Bless us with faithfulness and courage,
    that we may walk in the ways of Christ.
We ask these things in your holy name. Amen.

Words of Assurance (Ps 86, Matt 10)

Brothers and Sisters, hear the good news!
God forgives, redeems, and restores.
Believe in the good news
    and dwell in the promises of Christ.

Passing the Peace of Christ (Rom 6, Matt 10)

We are welcomed to this place by the one who rose from the dead and who brings us new life. In the name of Christ, greet one another with the peace and promise that comes from Jesus, the Christ.

Response to the Word (Gen 21, Matt 10)

Holy One, may we remember
    the stories of our ancestors.
May these stories become alive in us today,
    as we respond to your invitation to new life.
And may we be empowered to take up our cross
    and follow you. Amen.

Thanksgiving and Communion

Invitation to the Offering (Ps 86)

We come with joy and thanksgiving to this place because God's love abundantly provides for our needs.

Let us open our hearts and return to God a portion of our gifts, as we collect today's offering.

Offering Prayer (Gen 21, Ps 86)
>Generous God, as we offer these gifts to you,
>>we offer ourselves as well.
>May these gifts help our brothers and sisters,
>>both near and far.
>And may they be a sign of our steadfast faithfulness,
>>as we seek to live in your ways. Amen.

Sending Forth

Benediction (Gen 21, Matt 10)
>Brothers and sisters, go forth into the world,
>>knowing that God provides all that you need
>>to live abundantly with love and grace.
>Go forth, take up your cross, and follow Christ.
>Go in peace. Amen.

July 2, 2017

Fourth Sunday after Pentecost, Proper 8
Deborah Sokolove

Color

Green

Scripture Readings

Genesis 22:1-14; Psalm 13; Romans 6:12-23; Matthew 10:40-42

Theme Ideas

We do not always understand what God is asking of us. When we think we are called to a path of destruction, we meet God in surprising places and in ways that we do not expect. When we remain open and in relationship, we find eternal life in Christ.

Invitation and Gathering

Centering Words (Ps 13, Matt 10)
God's love is steadfast, inviting us to rejoice and find eternal life in love of God and others.

Call to Worship (Gen 22, Rom 6, Matt 10)
The Holy One calls us to trust God's steadfast love.
With our ancestor Abraham, we say:

> "Here I am."

The Holy One calls us to be guided by prophets.
With the first followers of Jesus, we say:

> "Here I am."

The Holy One calls us into eternal life.
With the Gospel writers, we say:

> "Here I am."

Let us worship the God who calls us.
Amen.

Opening Prayer (Matt 10)

Wellspring of Grace, Teacher of Truth,
Breath of Resurrection,
you welcome us into your life,
and invite us to welcome others
with a cup of water, a bite of bread,
a moment of conversation.
As we drink from the overflowing spring
of your endless love,
fill our hearts with thanksgiving and joy,
that we may become the body of Christ
pouring our lives into a world
that yearns to be filled. **Amen.**

Proclamation and Response

Prayer of Confession (Gen 22, Rom 6, Matt 10)

Teacher of Truth, you tell us to welcome
prophets and teachers,
and to give to those in need.
**Yet we want to hug your salvation to ourselves
and keep your gifts for our own use.**
You call us to be servants of your teaching,

and to remember that we are no longer slaves
to sin.
Yet we want to continue doing
what we have always done before,
hanging onto old habits and opinions,
even when you show us a better way.
You even offer us eternal life
when we surrender to your will.
Forgive us, Holy One,
when we mistake our will
for your own. Amen.

Words of Assurance (Rom 6)
God is a wellspring of grace,
offering the gift of eternal life
to all who do God's will.
In the name of Christ we are forgiven, loved, and free.
Thanks be to God. Amen.

Passing the Peace of Christ (Rom 6)
In gratitude for the gift of eternal life, let us greet one
another with signs of peace.
The peace of Christ be with you.
The peace of Christ be with you always.

Response to the Word (Rom 6, Matt 10)
Teacher of Truth, Breath of Resurrection,
Wellspring of Grace,
you have set us free from sin,
that we might know and do your will.
We welcome all who come in your name,
all who carry your good news
for the healing of the world.

Thanksgiving and Communion

Offering Prayer (Rom 6)
>Breath of Resurrection, Wellspring of Grace,
>>Teacher of Truth,
>>>we offer you these gifts
>>>>as tokens of our obedient hearts
>>>>>and of our desire to do your will. **Amen.**

Great Thanksgiving
>Christ be with you.
>>**And also with you.**
>Lift up your hearts.
>>**We lift them up to God.**
>Let us give our thanks to the Holy One.
>>**It is right to give our thanks and praise.**
>It is a right, good, and a joyful thing
>>always and everywhere to give our thanks to you,
>>who saved Abraham from sacrificing
>>his beloved son, Isaac,
>>and has given us the gift of eternal life in Christ.
>We give you thanks for freedom and friendship,
>>for love and for laughter,
>>for parents and children who travel together
>>in the ways of peace.
>We give you thanks for new understandings
>>of ancient stories,
>>for happy endings and new beginnings,
>>for cups of cold water on hot, sunny days.
>And so, with your creatures on earth
>>and all the heavenly chorus, we praise your name
>>and join their unending hymn:

Holy, holy, holy Lord, God of power and might,
  heaven and earth are full of your glory.
Hosanna in the highest. Blessed is the one
  who comes in the name of the Lord.
Hosanna in the highest.
Holy are you, and holy is your child, Jesus Christ,
  who taught his friends to spread the good news
  of freedom from evil, oppression, and violence,
  and who teaches us to welcome those
  who come in his name.
On the night in which he gave himself up,
  Jesus took bread, gave thanks to you,
  broke the bread, and gave it to the disciples, saying:
  "Take, eat; this is my body, which is given for you.
  Do this in remembrance of me."
When the supper was over, Jesus took the cup,
  offered thanks and gave it to the disciples, saying:
  "Drink from this, all of you;
  this is my life in the new covenant,
  poured out for you and for many,
  for the forgiveness of sins.
  Do this, as often as you drink it,
  in remembrance of me."
And so, in remembrance of your mighty acts
  in Jesus Christ, we proclaim the mystery of faith.
  Christ has died.
  Christ is risen.
  Christ will come again.
Pour out your Holy Spirit on us,
  and on these gifts of bread and wine.
Make them be for us the body and blood of Christ,
  that we may be the body of Christ
  to a world filled with temptations.

God of light and vision, God of mystery and truth,
God of love and grace,
we praise your saving, gracious name. **Amen.**

Sending Forth

Benediction (Matt 10)
With prophets and teachers,
and all who seek to do the will of God—
let us go forth to fill the empty cups of all who ask;
let us give in the name of the Breath of Resurrection,
the Wellspring of Grace, the Teacher of Truth:
the One, Triune God, who gives eternal life.
Amen.

July 9, 2017

Fifth Sunday after Pentecost, Proper 9
B. J. Beu

Color

Green

Scripture Readings

Genesis 24:34-38, 42-49, 58-67; Psalm 45:10-17; Romans 7:15-25a; Matthew 11:16-19, 25-30

Theme Ideas

"Proved to be right by her works" (Matthew 11:19). These words reveal the heart of putting our trust in God. In a strange country where he knew no one, Abraham's servant said to himself: "I'll have Isaac marry the first woman to give me a drink if she also offers to water my camels." Such a course seems like folly, and yet, Rebekah was that woman, and wisdom was vindicated by her deeds. Likewise, those who chose to follow Jesus willingly submitted to his yoke. Here again, wisdom revealed such action to be anything but folly. Truly, when following God, wisdom is vindicated by her deeds.

Invitation and Gathering

Centering Words (Gen 24, Matt 11)

Abraham's servant said to himself: "I'll have Isaac marry the first woman to give me a drink if she also offers to water my camels." Rebekah said to herself: "I'll leave my home with a perfect stranger, travel with him to a foreign country, and marry this man Isaac who I've never met. What could go wrong?" Such actions seem like folly, yet, wisdom is vindicated by her deeds.

Call to Worship (Matt 11)

Come to Christ, all who are weary
and carry heavy burdens.
     In Christ, we find rest.
Bear Christ's yoke and learn from him.
     In Christ, we find peace.
For Christ is gentle and humble in heart.
     In Christ, we find safety.
Christ's yoke is easy, and his burden light.
     In Christ, we find strength.
Come to Christ this day.
Wisdom is vindicated by her deeds.

Opening Prayer (Matt 11)

Welcomer of weary travelers,
     we have carried our burdens long
          and yearn to lay them down.
Give us your rest and your peace,
     even as we take your yoke upon us,
          for your yoke is easy,
               and your burden is light. Amen.

Proclamation and Response

Prayer of Confession (Rom 7, Matt 11)
God of mystery and wisdom beyond human reasoning,
    help us understand our own actions—
        for we do not do the things we want to do,
            but the very things we hate.
We observe our weakness,
    and we rebuke ourselves
        for our lack of will and resolve,
            yet we succumb to our destructive habits
                again and again.
Free us from feelings of self-loathing,
    and bless us with the strength and courage
        to embrace your yoke,
            that we may know
                the gentleness of your love,
                    and the depth of your mercy.
In Christ's name, we pray. Amen.

Words of Assurance (Rom 7, Matt 11)
Let all who feel lost and enslaved
    by self-destructive ways,
        turn to Christ Jesus, who is gentle of spirit
        and humble of heart.
For all who turn to Christ and accept his yoke
    find peace and fullness of grace.
Thanks be to God!

Passing the Peace of Christ (Matt 11)
All who lay down their burdens and take up Christ's yoke find rest and peace. Let us embrace this rest today as we inwardly turn to Christ, and outwardly share with one another the peace we have received.

Response to the Word (Gen 24, Matt 11)
Abraham's servant trusted God
and found Isaac a wife to comfort him
after the death of his mother.
Wisdom is vindicated by her deeds.
Rebekah trusted God, and became a matriarch
in the family of God's promised salvation.
Wisdom is vindicated by her deeds.
Followers of Christ put on Christ's yoke,
only to find rest and peace.
Truly, wisdom is vindicated by her deeds.

Thanksgiving and Communion

Invitation to the Offering (Gen 24)
As Abraham's servant showered Rebekah with gifts—
signs of the love that she would find in Isaac's household—so, too, may we offer our gifts to the world, as
signs of our love and commitment to God.

Offering Prayer (Ps 45, Matt 11)
God of overflowing generosity,
we celebrate your love
and praise your name.
May the gifts we return to you this day
turn the world's mourning and wailing
into singing and dancing,
through Jesus Christ,
our source of rest and peace. Amen.

Sending Forth

Benediction (Gen 24, Rom 7, Matt 11)
Go with the confidence of Rebekah,
who left security behind to trust the goodness of God.

Wisdom is vindicated by her deeds.
Go with the rest of weary travelers,
who trade their heaven burdens
for the peace and grace of Christ's yoke.
Wisdom is vindicated by her deeds.
Go with the joy and laughter
of those who dance and sing
with children in the marketplace.
Wisdom is vindicated by her deeds.
Go with God.

July 16, 2017

Sixth Sunday after Pentecost, Proper 10
Mary J. Scifres

Color

Green

Scripture Readings

Genesis 25:19-34; Psalm 119:105-112; Romans 8:1-11; Matthew 13:1-9, 18-23

Theme Ideas

Focusing on our priorities, on our spiritual well-being, and on following God's teachings leads to growth in the Spirit. When we lose focus, earthly matters and cares easily distract us. Once distracted, we draw away from the paths that bring fulfillment and lead to faithful discipleship. In various ways, the need for focus arises in all four of today's readings.

Invitation and Gathering

Centering Words (Rom 8, Matt 13)

Centered on God's Spirit, we come to nourish the soil of our lives. Planted in God's grace, we are prepared to grow in God's word as we live in the love of Christ.

Call to Worship (Matt 13)
> God scatters the seeds and calls us to grow.
>> **We come to grow in Christ.**
> God scatters the seeds and calls us to love.
>> **We come to love as Christ loves.**
> God scatters the seeds and calls us to hear.
>> **We come to listen for the word of God.**

Opening Prayer (Matt 13)
> Creator God, create fertile soil in lives.
> Plant your word in our hearts
>> and your wisdom in our souls.
> Open our minds to receive your insights
>> and your guidance.
> Nurture us this day,
>> that we may grow in mercy and grace
>>> all the days of our lives. Amen.

Proclamation and Response

Prayer of Confession (Matt 13)
> Great Sower of word and truth,
>> when we are confused,
>>> guide us with new understanding;
>> when we are distressed,
>>> help us be faithful and true;
>> when we are distracted,
>>> focus us with your Holy Spirit;
>> when we are worried,
>>> comfort us with your blessed assurance.
> Nourish the soil of our lives,
>> that we may be fertile recipients of your word
>>> and faithful followers of Christ Jesus.
> In your mercy and love, we pray. Amen.

Words of Assurance (Rom 8:1-2)

There isn't any condemnation in Christ Jesus.
The Spirit of life in Christ Jesus
    has set us free from the law of sin and death.
In this new law of loving grace,
    we are forgiven and free!

Introduction to the Word or Call to Worship (Matt 13)

God scatters the seeds and calls us to grow.
We come to grow in Christ.
God scatters the seeds and calls us to hear.
We will listen for the word of God.

Response to the Word (Matt 13)

Seeds have been scattered; words have been spoken.
We are ready to bear much fruit.
Water is needed; the soil must be tended.
We will nurture one another well.
God has scattered the seeds and sends us to love.
We will go to share the love of Christ.

Thanksgiving and Communion

Offering Prayer (Matt 13)

Gardener God, bless these gifts
    that we return to you now.
May they become seeds of hope
    that bear the fruit of your love
        in the ministries and missions we share.

Invitation to Communion (Matt 13)

The Gardener is here—ready to sow seeds of love, ready
to nourish us as we grow, ready to feed us on the journey of life and faith. Come, this meal is God's gift of
nourishment and growth for us, and for all those who
follow the Sower.

Communion Prayer (Matt 13)
  Pour out your Holy Spirit on us,
    that the seeds you have planted
      may flourish and grow.
  Pour out your Holy Spirit
    on these gifts of bread and wine,
      that they may become signs of your life and love,
        living and growing in us.
  By your grace and strength,
    make us the fruit of your harvest,
      your presence of love and justice here on earth.
  As we grow in your Spirit,
    make us one with you, one with each other,
    and one in ministry to all the world,
      until Christ comes in final victory
        and we feast at the heavenly banquet.
  Through Jesus Christ,
    with the Holy Spirit in your holy Church,
      all honor and glory is yours, Almighty God,
        now and forevermore. Amen.

Giving the Bread and Cup
  (The bread and wine are given to the people, with these or other words of blessing.)
  The harvest of God for the people of God.
  The fruit of the Spirit for the people of God's Spirit.

Sending Forth

Benediction (Matt 13)
  Go to be seeds of Christ's love.
  Go to scatter seeds of God's hope.
  Go to bear the fruit of God's Holy Spirit.

July 23, 2017

Seventh Sunday after Pentecost, Proper 11
Safiyah Fosua

Color

Green

Scripture Readings

Genesis 28:10-19a; Psalm 139:1-12, 23-24; Romans 8:12-25; Matthew 13:24-30, 36-43

Theme Ideas

The Genesis text and the text from Matthew are profound examples of grace. In Genesis, Jacob receives a heavenly vision after an act of cowardice. His visit to Rebekah's kin to take a wife was more of a ruse to save him from being murdered by his brother than a mission to find love. In Matthew, the weeds are allowed to grow in the field for a time, though they are more worthy of the fire. The two texts are tied together by the hopeful reminder of Psalm 139: God knows all about us, yet loves us still.

Invitation and Gathering

Centering Words (Ps 139)

God is neither shocked nor disturbed by our imperfections. God, who is already familiar with our ways, has called us to this place.

Call to Worship

Stand and bear witness
to the fulfillment of God's promise:
We are those descendants,
too many to count...
Like the dust of the earth.
Like the sands of the beach.
Like the stars in the heavens.
We are those descendants,
too many to count...
From the West and the East.
From the North and the South.
Too many to count...
From the Atlantic and the Pacific.
From Antarctica and Australia.
Too many to count...
From Canada to Côte d'Ivoire.
From New York to Nairobi.
We are those descendants,
too many to count...
Blessed of God.
Blessed to be a blessing.

Opening Prayer (Gen 28)

God of our mothers and our fathers,
God of ages past, God of all our tomorrows,
we have come here at your invitation.

We come, as companions on a journey,
     through this howling wilderness called life.
We are a motley, mixed multitude.
Some of us are on top of the world,
     and others of us have been wearied
          by the ordinariness of our days.
Yet we all long for something new.
Surprise us with a glimpse of your presence,
     just as you surprised the prophet Isaiah long ago,
          and just as you surprised Jacob
               on the road to Haran.
Open our eyes, O God,
     to a fresh vision of your love.
Open our hearts,
     that we might sense your presence
          and be healed today. **Amen**.

Proclamation and Response

Prayer of Confession (Gen 28, Ps 139, Matt 13)
     God of the heavenly stair, we are imperfect people,
          longing for a glimpse of your glory.
     We are like Jacob,
          praying for a fresh start
               after a past that still makes us blush.
     When we consider the field of our hearts,
          we hope to be deemed more *wheat* than *weed*
               when the day of reckoning comes.
     With the psalmist, we ask you to examine our hearts,
          and make our imperfections known to us,
               that we might have the courage to change

and become the people
you envision us to be.
(Silence)

Words of Assurance (1 John 1)
Receive the good news:
God, who is faithful and just,
forgives those who sincerely confess their sins.
Hear this good news:
We worship a God of forgiveness,
not condemnation.

Response to the Word (Gen 28, Matt 13)
Who among us is worthy of God's blessings?
For we are like Jacob—
running to escape our past.
Who among us is worthy of God's blessings?
For we are a fickle field—
wheat one day, weeds the next.
Who among us is worthy of God's blessings?
Lord, make us worthy!

Thanksgiving and Communion

Offering Prayer (Gen 28)
God, just as you received Jacob's gift
of oil poured on the stone that had been his pillow,
receive our humble gifts today
as an act of worship.
May our offering make your name known
in places where you are needed. Amen.

Sending Forth

Benediction
God promised that every family of the earth
would be blessed through God's people.
You are blessed to be a blessing.
You have been blessed.
Now go and *be* a blessing! Amen.

July 30, 2017

Eighth Sunday after Pentecost, Proper 12
B. J. Beu & Mary J. Scifres

Color

Green

Scripture Readings

Genesis 29:15-28; Psalm 105:1-11, 45b; Romans 8:26-39; Matthew 13:31-33, 44-52

Theme Ideas

Good things come to those who wait. Or as Paul puts it: "All things work together for good for the ones who love God, for those who are called according to [God's] purposes" (8:28). Today's scriptures encourage us to trust that God's realm is worth waiting for. Laban tricks Jacob into marrying Leah rather than Rachel, but without this first marriage, we would not have ten of the twelve tribes of Israel. Waiting in prayer, we discover that the Spirit prays for us even when we cannot. Waiting for seeds to become trees, and yeast to become risen bread, we see how waiting with God and growing with God can bring God's realm here on earth.

Invitation and Gathering

Centering Words (Matt 13, Rom 8)
Waiting is seldom easy. Yet, in the process of waiting, we discover new growth. The Spirit moves and breathes, and treasures are sometimes discovered. As we wait this day, may God's miraculous presence be revealed in us and through us.

Call to Worship (Ps 105, Rom 8)
Waiting and hoping, we gather together,
seeking God's presence and singing God's praise.
Waiting and hoping, we come now to worship,
praying and listening for the Spirit's guidance.
Waiting and hoping, we gather together,
seeking God's presence and singing God's praise.

Opening Prayer (Matt 13
Holy One, your kingdom always takes us by surprise—
like a mustard seed growing into a great shrub
where the birds of the air
can build their nests;
like a treasure hidden in a field,
or a pearl of great price.
May we desire your kingdom
more than we value worldly things,
through Christ, who shows us the way. Amen.

Proclamation and Response

Prayer of Confession (Gen 29, Ps 105, Rom 8, Matt 13)
Eternal God, waiting is hard—
waiting for justice,

waiting for peace,
waiting for love,
waiting for your presence to heal us.
Give us the patience and passion of Jacob,
    to work for the deepest desire of our hearts.
Give us the perseverance of Abraham,
    to keep going when all hope seems lost.
Transform our hope into action,
    that we may help build your kingdom
        here on earth. Amen.

Words of Assurance (Rom 8:38-39 NRSV)
Nothing can separate us from the love of God:
    Not death, nor life, nor angels, nor rulers,
    nor things present, nor things to come.
No power on heaven or under the earth
can separate us from the love of Christ:
    Not height, nor depth,
    nor anything else in all creation.
    Thanks be to God!

Passing the Peace of Christ (Rom 8)
Nothing in all of creation can separate us from the love
and peace of God in Jesus Christ. Let us share this love
and peace with one another today.

Response to the Word (Gen 29, Ps 105, Rom 8)
All things work together for good
for those who love God.
    Working for love builds a future
    for the whole family of God.
All things work together for good
for those who wait for God.

> **Waiting for the stirring of Spirit,**
> **seeds grow into trees and treasures are revealed.**
> All things work together for good
> for those who love God and know how to wait.

Thanksgiving and Communion

Invitation to the Offering (Rom 8, Matt 13)

God's kingdom is like treasure hidden in a field. Through today's offering, we can help others find treasure in their lives—treasure that is there only through our giving. Come enter into the mystery of kingdom building and treasure hunting as we collect today's offering.

Offering Prayer (Ps 105, Matt 13)

Giver of all good gifts,
    help us be kingdom builders
        as we offer our gifts to the world.
May our gifts be like treasure in a field
    for those waiting for new life.
May our offerings be like yeast
    for those hungering for their daily bread.
Bless our lives and our giving,
    that we might be part of the great mystery
        of kingdom building,
            in world waiting to be remade. Amen.

Communion Prayer (Matt 13)

Bakerwoman God,
    bless this gift of bread
        with the yeast of your love;
    flow through this gift of wine
        with the Spirit of your grace.

Nurture our lives,
   that we may be loaves
      of your generous abundance
         and vines of your growth and strength.
In Christ's name, we pray. Amen.

Sending Forth

Benediction (Matt 13)
   Like treasure hidden in a field,
   Christ offers us the kingdom of God.
   All things work together for good
   for those who love God.
   Like a pearl of great price,
   Christ offers us the kingdom of heaven.
   All things work together for good
   for those who wait for God.
   Like a mustard seed that grows into a great shrub,
   Christ offers us the realm of God's blessing.
   All things work together for good
   for those who abide in God's Spirit.

August 6, 2017

Ninth Sunday after Pentecost, Proper 13
Joanne Carlson Brown

Color

Green

Scripture Readings

Genesis 32:22-31; Psalm 17:1-7, 15; Romans 9:1-15; Matthew 14:13-21

Theme Ideas

It is an awesome thing to encounter God face to face. It can shake us to our very core. And of one thing we can be sure, we will never be the same again. On this anniversary of Hiroshima, we wrestle with our conscience, our very faith in humanity and, indeed, in God. How could we do such a thing? In this wrestling, we come to a conviction that never again will we participate in or celebrate such massive destruction and loss of life. We limp along on our journey to reaffirm our humanity, turning to see the face of God and feeling the strength that comes through our encounter with God. For this God loves us unconditionally and is with us every step we take on our journey of discovery, repentance, and faith.

Invitation and Gathering

Centering Words (Ps 17)

As for me, I shall behold your face....When I awake I
shall be satisfied, beholding your likeness.

Call to Worship (Gen 32, Ps 17)

Why have you come this morning?
We have come to encounter the Holy One.
You know you'll never be the same if you do.
We have come to wrestle with our faith,
our doubts, and even our convictions.
Then come; let us venture into this time of worship
and prepare to encounter God face to face.
(Leads into "Come, O Thou Traveler Unknown")

Opening Prayer (Gen 32, Ps 17)

O God of nighttime visits and daylight assurance,
we come to this time of worship
to wrestle with who we are,
and who you call us to be.
Search our hearts and know us thoroughly.
We long to meet you face to face,
even if the encounter leaves us forever changed.
With open ears and ready hearts,
touch us with your words
and transform us with your presence. Amen.

Proclamation and Response

Prayer of Confession (Gen 32, Ps 17)

God who sees, knows, and touches us,
we have many things in our lives
that we are not proud of.

We are scared to come before you
>with all that we are.
We are frightened that you will judge us
>and find us wanting.
We are afraid of your rejection or abandonment.
Forgive our shortcomings, large and small.
Reassure us that you are always present with us,
>that you always love us
>>and want only the best for us.
Forgive our fearful reluctance to open ourselves fully
>to an encounter with your holy presence.
Wrestle with us, touch us,
>and awaken us to your love—
>>a love that never lets us go.
Meet us face to face,
>that we may be forever changed. Amen.

Words of Assurance (Gen 32, Ps 17)
>Dawn comes, and we will see God face to face.
>We will behold the face of unconditional love.
>In this meeting, we will understand the depth
>>of God's reassuring forgiveness.
>And in this understanding,
>>we will be changed for good.

Response to the Word (Gen 32, Ps 17)
>Your word wrestles with us,
>>and we engage it with all our heart
>>>and mind and strength.
>May we be forever changed
>>by the encounter with you, O God,
>>>in these words.

Thanksgiving and Communion

Offering Prayer (Gen 32, Ps 17)
We have much to offer,
    because we have received much from your hands,
        loving and caring God.
We are satisfied with what we have been given,
    and out of this satisfaction,
        we give these offerings back to you
            through your church.
May our material resources
    be matched by the offering we make of ourselves,
        that the world may be changed, as we have been,
            through encounter with you. Amen.

Sending Forth

Benediction (Gen 32, Ps 17)
Go forth, knowing that God has heard our cry
    and will give us the strength to follow God's call.
Go forth to touch the lives of others,
    as our lives have been touched by God.
Go and be the face of God
    to a world that so desperately needs
        the loving, affirming face of God.
And may the wrestling God be with you always. Amen.

Additional Resource

Litany For Hiroshima Memorial Day
A flash of brilliant light,
a mushroom cloud rises.

Nothing will ever be the same.
We dedicate ourselves to work for peace
as we boldly proclaim:
"Never again."
Forgive our inhumanity.
May wars cease as we work to be peacemakers
and not merely peace hopers.
Touch us, O God, and we will never be the same.
In life and in death we are not alone.
Thanks be to God.

August 13, 2017

Tenth Sunday after Pentecost, Proper 14
B. J. Beu
[Copyright © 2016 by B. J. Beu. Used by permission.]

Color

Green

Scripture Readings

Genesis 37:1-4, 12-28; Psalm 105:1-6, 16-22, 45b; Romans
10:5-15; Matthew 14:22-33

Theme Ideas

Even in the midst of our failings, God can turn human
weakness into acts of deliverance. Genesis 37 begins the
story of Joseph's sale into slavery by his brothers. Psalm
105 proclaims that God used this act of betrayal to deliv-
er the world from the ravages of famine. Paul proclaims
that all who profess Christ with their lips and who believe in him with their whole hearts will be saved. Matthew 14 recalls the story of Peter's fear and doubt as he
walks on the water toward Jesus.

Invitation and Gathering

Centering Words (Gen 37, Ps 105, Matt 14)

When winds howl and seas rage, Christ beckons us from the storm, calling us to walk in faith. When circumstances break against us, God transforms our misfortunes into blessings. The mysteries of God are deeper than the foundations of the earth.

Call to Worship (Gen 37, Ps 105, Rom 10)

Rejoice in the Lord.
Call on God's holy name.
Give thanks to the Lord.
Sing to our God with shouts of joy.
Rejoice in the Lord.
Proclaim God's mighty works.
Give thanks to the Lord.
Proclaim the miracles of God's hands.
Rejoice in the Lord.
Trust in God's saving love.
Give thanks to the Lord.
Tell the wonders of God's glory.

Opening Prayer (Gen 37, Ps 105, Rom 10:15 (NRSV), Matt 14)

Eternal God, in visions and dreams,
your offer us hope for a new tomorrow.
Amidst life's storms and raging waters,
be with us in our time of need.
Reveal to us the great works we are capable of,
that we may rise above our narrow purposes,
and be of service to the world.
Bless our journeys,

that it may be said of us:
  "How beautiful are the feet
    of those who bring good news!"

Proclamation and Response

Prayer of Confession (Gen 37, Matt 14)
God of the lost and forsaken,
  without your aid we are powerless
    and are quickly beaten by the storms of life;
  without your grace we fall to our injuries
    and are soon imprisoned by our resentments;
  without your intervention we quickly submerge
    and gasp for breath in our misery and despair.
Reacquaint us with your saving grace,
  that we may know that anything is possible,
    even when everything is falling apart.
Renew our dreams and hopes for the future,
  that we may be instruments of your promise,
    even when the whole world seems against us.
Amen.

Assurance of Pardon (Rom 10, Matt 14)
Everyone who calls on the name of the Lord
  will be saved.
Everyone who risks the uncertain walk of faith,
  receives aid from the one who calms the waters.

Passing the Peace (Rom 10)
It is said: "How beautiful are the feet of those who come proclaiming peace." May our sanctuary be filled with extraordinary beauty as we share the peace of Christ today.

Response to the Word (Gen 37, Ps 105, Matt 14)
Brothers betray brothers,
yet God remains faithful.
Families turn their back on their own,
yet God remains true.
Believers sink in the waters of fear and doubt,
yet God remains our firm foundation.
When all other help vanishes,
God remains. Thanks be to God.

Thanksgiving and Communion

Offering Prayer (Ps 105, Matt 14)
We praise you, O Lord,
for your wonderful works.
As we bring our offerings before you this day,
we rejoice in your saving love
with hearts full of song.
May our offering be a sign of our pledge
to walk faithfully before you,
each and every day of our lives. Amen.

Sending Forth

Benediction (Gen 37, Ps 105, Matt 14)
God blesses us with strength for the journey.
Christ lifts us up from the raging waters of life.
The Spirit guides us with dreams and visions
of a glorious tomorrow.
Go with God.

August 20, 2017

Eleventh Sunday after Pentecost, Proper 15
Mary J. Scifres
[Copyright © 2016 by Mary J. Scifres. Used by permission.]

Color

Green

Scripture Readings

Genesis 45:1-15; Psalm 133; Romans 11:1-2a, 29-32; Matthew 15:(10-20) 21-28

Theme Ideas

Mercy flows through today's readings: from Joseph's forgiving words to his brothers, to the psalmist's rejoicing over unity, to Paul's reminder to the Romans of God's mercy. Jesus reminds us that words and attitudes are more precious than perfect ritual. But, as he is confronted by a Canaanite woman, even Jesus needs reminding that mercy comes first. Jesus responds with both healing and admiration of her great perseverance and faith.

Invitation and Gathering

Centering Words (Rom 11, Ps 23)

May mercy and grace follow us this day and all the days of our lives.

Call to Worship (Ps 133)
How good it is when we gather in unity and love.
How beautiful is this body of Christ.
How good it is when we gather in mercy and grace.
How beautiful is the love we have come to share.

Opening Prayer (Gen 45, Ps 133, Rom 11, Matt 15)
Merciful God, thank you for gathering us
    in your grace and love this day.
Bless us with compassion and understanding,
    that we may be people of forgiveness
        and acceptance.
Strengthen us with the power of your Holy Spirit,
    that we may be unified in mercy and grace for all.
In Christ's mercy and grace, we pray. Amen.

Proclamation and Response

Prayer of Confession (Gen 45, Rom 11, Matt 15)
Forgiving God,
    you know when we withhold forgiveness.
Merciful One,
    you know when we are not merciful.
Gracious Christ,
    you know when we are stingy with your grace.
Acceptor and Lover of all,
    you know when we reject and exclude.
Forgive us and reclaim us.
Strengthen us with your Spirit of love,
    that we may offer forgiveness and compassion
        in the pursuit of your unity and love.
In your mercy and grace, we pray. Amen.

Words of Assurance (Rom 11)
God, who is merciful to all, forgives us all
through the grace and compassion of Christ.

Passing the Peace of Christ (Ps 133)
How beautiful it is when the family of God lives together in unity and peace! Let us share that beauty with one another as we share the love and peace of Christ today.

Introduction to the Word (Matt 15)
Let us feed our hearts and souls with the word of God as we look for guidance this day.

Response to the Word (Gen 45, Ps 133, Matt 15)
Where forgiveness is needed,
forgive our sins, as we forgive others.
Where grace is yearned for,
may we know grace upon grace,
and show the same to one another.
Where mercy is required,
may Christ's mercy flow through us,
that others may find mercy in us.
Where unity is threatened,
may your Spirit strengthen us
to be people of unity and love.

Thanksgiving and Communion

Invitation to the Offering (Ps 133)
How beautiful it is when the family of God gives generously with mercy and love! Let us share that beauty with the world as we collect our offering this day.

Offering Prayer (Rom 11, Matt 15)
> Bless these gifts, O God,
>> that they may bring mercy and grace,
>>> compassion and love, and healing and hope,
>>>> through the ministries and missions
>>>>> we support.
> In Christ's gracious name, we pray. Amen.

Sending Forth

Benediction (Rom 11)
> Go in God's mercy and grace.
>> **We will share God's mercy and grace.**
> Go in Christ's peace and love.
>> **We will share Christ's peace and love.**
> Go and be a blessing to the world.

August 27, 2017

Twelfth Sunday after Pentecost, Proper 16
B. J. Beu
[Copyright © 2016 by B. J. Beu. Used by permission.]

Color

Green

Scripture Readings

Exodus 1:8–2:10; Psalm 124; Romans 12:1-8; Matthew 16:13-20

Theme Ideas

It takes a village. Each person has a role to play to bring the realm of God. It took a village of women (the midwives Shiphrah and Puah, Moses' mother and sister, and the daughter of Pharaoh) to birth, protect, and raise Moses, the leader who would lead the Hebrew people from slavery and oppression. It took Peter and the other disciples to proclaim the good news after Jesus' death. It took people with many and diverse spiritual gifts to imbue the church with the talents it needed to thrive. Each of us has an important role to bring the kingdom of God among us. Truly, it takes a village.

Invitation and Gathering

Centering Words (Ps 124)

If it had not been the Lord who was on our side, when the storms of life came crashing down upon us, we would have been lost. Despite all our cleverness, despite all our careful planning and calculated moves, if it had not been the Lord who was on our side, all our efforts would have been in vain.

Call to Worship (Exod 1–2)

Amidst the forces of death and destruction,
it takes a village to save us.
Amidst the rivers that would carry us out to sea,
it takes people of real courage
to pull us from the water courses of life.
Amidst the fear and hatred in our world,
it takes mercy and compassion
to reveal the face of God.
Come, let us worship.

Opening Prayer (Rom 12)

Gracious God, we come this day,
to present our minds and bodies to you
as a holy and living sacrifice.
We seek the blessings that come
from the renewal of our minds.
May we discern your will
and come to know what is good
and acceptable and perfect in your sight. Amen.

Proclamation and Response

Prayer of Confession (Exod 1–2)
Merciful God, wash away the injuries
we have inflicted upon one another.
When we have made lives bitter
through word or deed,
forgive us in your mercy.
When we have ignored the plight of others
through ignorance or willful neglect,
reclaim us in your grace.
Restore us to your path of love and compassion,
that we may bathe in the waters
of your compassion and love. Amen.

Words of Assurance (Ps 124)
If it had not been the Lord who was on our side,
the weight of the world
would have crushed us by now.
If it had not been the Lord who was on our side,
the weight of our lives
would have drowned us by now.
Thanks be to God who is on our side,
and who rescues us from forces
that seek our undoing.
In Christ Jesus, we are set free
and made whole again.

Passing the Peace (Rom 12, Matt 16)
When we recognize Christ for who he really is, we find
the peace and security to see ourselves for who we really are. Let us share this peace with one another as we
pass the peace of Christ.

Response to the Word (Exod 1–2, Rom 12)
God of mercy and compassion, hear our prayer.
As you heard the cries of Moses in the river Nile,
    hear the cries of those who suffer injustice today.
As you moved the heart of Pharaoh's daughter
    to save the young Hebrew child,
        move our hearts to save the lives of those
            who cannot help themselves.
Bind us together into a village of love and support,
    that we might saves your children
        from death and destruction.
May the work of our hands
    and the meditations of our hearts
        help build your kingdom here on earth. Amen.

Thanksgiving and Communion

Invitation to the Offering (Exod 1–2, Rom 12, Matt 16)
God's light shines through our giving hearts and our
generous spirits. Christ's voice calls us to heal the
wounded and to keep the forces of death at bay. In our
sharing, let us bring the kingdom to a world in need.

Offering Prayer (Exod 1–2, Rom 12)
Loving God, accept our gifts in your holy name.
Accept our very lives,
    as a pledge to pursue what is good
        and acceptable and perfect in your sight.
May our gifts become for the world
    resources to draw the endangered
        from the waters of death,
            through Jesus Christ our Lord. Amen.

Sending Forth

Benediction (Exod 1–2, Mark 16)
>   Blessed are you who resist the forces
>   of death and destruction.
>   Blessed are you who respond to the cries of the weak
>   and the helpless.
>   Blessed are you who build the kingdom of God
>   with your love and compassion.
>   Blessed are you who seek first
>   what is right and honorable and true.

September 3, 2017

Thirteenth Sunday after Pentecost, Proper 17
Mary J. Scifres

Color

Green

Scripture Readings

Exodus 3:1-15; Psalm 105:1-6, 23-26, 45c; Romans 12:9-21; Matthew 16:21-28

Theme Ideas

Love and serve. Serve with love. Serve because of love. These themes emerge in all of today's readings, but most emphatically in Romans 12. The challenge to love with total empathy and compassion is surely as challenging as carrying one's cross. It may even be the only way we can carry our crosses once we have decided to follow Christ.

Invitation and Gathering

Centering Words (Rom 12, Matt 16)
Serve first, last, and always—even when you get nothing back in return. Love without limit—be it enemy,

friend or stranger. For it is in serving and loving that we carry our crosses and become true disciples of Christ's love.

Call to Worship
> In mutual compassion and authentic love...
> > **we gather as the family of God.**
> We offer our gifts, our hope, and our lives...
> > **to build up this community of faith.**
> We bring our songs of gratitude and joy...
> > **to bless God with our worship and praise.**

Opening Prayer (Ps 105, Rom 12)
> Loving God, we come in search of you
> > and your loving wisdom.
> Come to us and gather us in your love.
> Mold us into a community of compassion
> > that is strengthened by the unity and power
> > > of your Holy Spirit.
> In joyous gratitude, we pray. Amen.

Proclamation and Response

Prayer of Confession (Rom 12, Matt 16)
> God of peace, have mercy on us.
> We have created divisions among ourselves,
> > even though you call us to live in peace.
> We have given in to hatred, vengeance, enmity, and evil,
> > even though you call us to serve and to love.
> Servant God, give us hearts that overflow
> > with love, compassion, and service,
> > > that we may offer forgiveness as freely
> > > > as you have offered it to us;

and that we may give as freely
as you have given to us.
In your amazing love, we pray. Amen.

Words of Assurance (Ps 105, Rom 12)

Remember the wonderful works of God,
the amazing peace of Christ,
and the powerful love of the Spirit.
For in this Holy Trinity of grace,
we are forgiven, reunited, and reconciled
with God and with one another.

Passing the Peace of Christ (Rom 12)

Live at peace with all people to the best of your ability.
With this hope and this prayer, let us share words of
love and signs of reconciliation as we pass the peace of
Christ.

Introduction to the Word (Ps 105)

In pursuit of God, we come now to listen. As we seek
God's face, we come now to look. Listen and hear, not
just with your ears, but with your hearts and minds.
For the One who is present in all places and at all times
comes to us in many ways.

Response to the Word

Take up your cross and follow Christ.
We will follow with love and compassion.
Set aside selfish ways and serve with Christ.
We will serve with love and compassion.
Forsake vengeance and rejoice in forgiveness.
We will persevere in love and compassion.

Thanksgiving and Communion

Invitation to the Offering (Rom 12:13)

Contribute to the needs of God's people. Welcome strangers into this church home. These calls of hospitality are answered when we give of our time, talent, and treasure. Let us offer our gifts to God this day.

Offering Prayer (Ps 105, Rom 12)

Creator God, in remembrance of your wonderful works
and your overflowing abundance,
we bring gifts that we have received
from your hand.
Generous One, in gratitude for your miraculous deeds,
we bring these offerings of praise.
Loving Spirit, in joyous trust,
we place these blessings in your keeping
to bless a world in need of your love.

Great Thanksgiving (Rom 12)

Lift up your hearts!
We lift them up to God!
Celebrate God's love!
It is right to give our thanks and praise!
We give thanks and praise to you,
God of love and grace!
With gratitude, we recall how your formed us
from the very earth, made covenant with us
from the beginning of time,
and call us again and again to be your people.
In your amazing love, you came as one of us
in the form of Jesus the Christ,

showing us the way of unconditional love
and the path of self-giving service.
(You may choose to add here the Sanctus, "Holy, Holy, Holy Lord,").
Even as he faced death on a cross,
Jesus washed the feet of both enemies and friends,
gave thanks and rejoiced in a time of great sorrow,
broke bread and shared the cup of salvation with all,
showing us the path of servanthood and love.
And so we remember Jesus' words of self-giving love
as he broke bread and poured wine, saying:
"Take, eat, this is my body, broken for you.
Take, drink. This is my life poured out for you
and for many for the forgiveness of sins."
Called to remember these acts whenever we eat
and drink, we come now to the table
in remembrance of these gifts
as we proclaim the mystery of faith.
Christ has died.
Christ is risen.
Christ will come again.

Communion Prayer (Rom 12)

God of love, pour out your Holy Spirit on us,
that we might be servants of your love.
Pour out your Holy Spirit
on these gifts of bread and wine,
that they might be for us your very presence.
Flow through us with your love and grace,
that we might be your loving presence for others,
extending kindness to strangers,
forgiveness to adversaries,
and mutual love to all.

Live in us, that by your Spirit,
  we might be one with Christ,
    one with each other,
      and one in ministry to all the world,
        until Christ comes in final victory
          and we feast at the heavenly banquet.
Through Jesus Christ,
  and with the Holy Spirit in your holy Church,
    all honor and glory is yours, Almighty God,
      both now and forever more. Amen.

Giving the Bread and Cup
(The bread and wine are given to the people, with these or other words of blessing.)
The life of Christ, fitting your life for service.
The love of God, blessing your care for the world

Sending Forth

Benediction (Rom 12, Matt 16)
Love, as Jesus has loved you.
  We go to serve, as Jesus served.
Go with the peace that passes all understanding.
  We go to heal the world, as Jesus healed.

September 10, 2017

Fourteenth Sunday after Pentecost, Proper 18
Mary Petrina Boyd

Color

Green

Scripture Readings

Exodus 12:1-14; Psalm 149; Romans 13:8-14; Matthew 18:15-20

Theme Ideas

These scriptures reflect on what it means to lead a faithful life. Exodus describes the Passover meal, where Hebrews living under harsh Egyptian rule prepare to leave bondage on the journey to freedom. First they must prepare, then they must remember. Psalm 149 begins with a celebration of God and then moves to a call to overthrow the tyrants that enslave God's people. Romans reminds us to obey the commandments, particularly the commandment to love. Matthew calls followers to the holy life of community, promising the presence of Jesus in their midst.

Invitation and Gathering

Centering Words (Exod 12, Rom 13)

We are called to love one another, to answer God's invitation, and to walk in the light of God's love.

Call to Worship (Rom 13)

The time is near!

The night is past.

Leave the darkness behind.

Live in the light of God's love.

Set aside selfish ways.

Share Christ's love wherever you are.

The time is near!

Let us worship God.

—Or—

Call to Worship (Ps 149)

Praise the Lord.

Sing to the Lord a new song.

Celebrate God's goodness.

Praise God with music.

Rejoice in God's love.

Shout for joy.

Praise the Lord.

Opening Prayer (Exod 12, Ps 149, Rom 13, Matt 18)

Holy God, we sing your songs of praise,

rejoicing in your love.

We know that when we gather,

you are here with us.

Build us into a faithful community—

a community that cares for one another
and listens to one another in love.
Living your law of love,
help us follow you onto new paths. Amen

Proclamation and Response

Prayer of Confession (Exod 12, Rom 13)
God of freedom, you help us leave behind
all that keeps us from being fully human,
yet we resist your help
and the change you offer.
Clinging to old, familiar patterns,
we are reluctant to move on.
When others challenge us,
we grow defensive.
Give us open and generous hearts,
that we may hear your call
and follow you on new adventures
of love and compassion. Amen.

Words of Assurance (Exod 12, Matt 18)
Jesus promises that if two agree and ask,
God hears our prayers and grants our request.
Together, let us forgive what is past
and ask God to lead us into a future of hope.

Passing the Peace of Christ (Matt 18:20)
Jesus promises: "Where two or three are gathered in my
name, I'm there with them." Christ is with us now. With
joy and thanksgiving, greet one another as fellow children of God.

Response to the Word (Exod 12, Rom 13)
Gracious God, give us the courage to answer your call.
Give us the wisdom to ask for your direction.
Give us the purity of heart to love as you have loved us.

Thanksgiving and Communion

Invitation to the Offering (Rom 13)
Our only obligation is to love God and one another. Let
us give with generous hearts, sharing our love with our
neighbors.

Offering Prayer (Rom 13)
God of light and love, you provide all that we need.
As first you gave the gift of life and love to us,
    so now we bring our gifts to you.
May they reflect the love and concern
    we have for our neighbors.
May they represent our commitment
    to build communities of freedom and hope. Amen.

Sending Forth

Benediction (Exod 12, Rom 13, Matt 18)
Put your sandals on your feet
    and take your staff in your hand.
Walk away from darkness
    and enter the joy and love of God's love.
Follow God's call.
    for Christ is with you.
Go in peace and joy.

September 17, 2017

Fifteenth Sunday after Pentecost, Proper 19
B. J. Beu

Color

Green

Scripture Readings

Exodus 14:19-31; Exodus 15:1b-11, 20-21; Romans 14:1-12; Matthew 18:21-35

Theme Ideas

Rescue and rejoicing tie today's Exodus readings together. Forgiveness and refraining from judgment tie today's epistle and Gospel readings together. Redemption and reclamation further unify the Exodus and epistle readings—for both are God's gifts to the Hebrew people, just as they are Christ's gifts to the Christian community. In the Exodus story, God rescues the people from Pharaoh, and Miriam leads the rejoicing of her people. God redeems the Israelites from slavery and claims them as the people of God. Likewise, in the epistle to the Romans, Christ redeems us and claims us as God's own children.

Invitation and Gathering

Centering Words (Exod 14, 15)

If it had not been the Lord who was on our side when the forces of death pressed against us, we would have no songs to sing to our children. If it had not been the Lord who was on our side when the instruments of death had us in their power, we would be the victims of the unrighteous. Sing to our God, who brings us into a future of hope and life.

Call to Worship (Exod 14, 15; Rom 14)

Sing to God for mercy and grace.
Sing praises to God for laughter and joy.
For our God is mighty and strong,
protecting the lowly from the anger of the oppressor.
Our God is righteous and just,
saving the weak from the cruelty of the powerful.
Sing to God for mercy and grace.
Sing praises to God for laughter and joy.

Opening Prayer (Exod 14, 15; Rom 14)

Gracious God, renew our minds and cleanse our spirits,
that we might rise above the petty judgments
that keep us from full fellowship
with you and with one another.
Part the waters of our worries and confusion,
and save us from the tides
that threaten to overwhelm us.
Be merciful to us and protect us with your powerful hand,
that we might dance and sing to your glory. Amen.

Proclamation and Response

Prayer of Confession (Exod 14, 15; Rom 14)
Merciful God,
> when we have inflicted injuries upon others,
>> forgive us;
>
> when we have laughed and sung
>> as our enemies faced calamity,
>>> pardon us;
>
> when we have belittled the convictions of others
>> through word or deed,
>>> restore us in your mercy.

Reclaim us, Mighty One,
> that amidst the trials of life,
>> we might walk on the dry land
>>> of your powerful hope
>>>> and your loving grace,
>>>>> through Jesus Christ, our Lord. Amen.

Words of Assurance (Exod 14, 15)
If it had not been the Lord who was on our side,
> the forces of death would have claimed us as victims.

If it had not been the Lord who was on our side,
> we would have fallen to the sword
> or been drowned by the sea.

Dance and sing to the Lord who is on our side,
> and is on the side of all God's children.

Passing the Peace (Exod 14, 15; Rom 14)
We live not for ourselves, but for the One who rescues us from peril and calls us into fellowship with one another. Let us give thanks for the love of God, as we share signs of Christ's peace this day.

Response to the Word (Exod 14, 15; Rom 14)

Send your Messenger, Holy One,
> to guide our steps through the waters of fear
>> onto the dry land of your promised salvation.

Open our mouths with laughter and song,
> as we rejoice in our deliverance.

But let our eyes flow with tears,
> as we mourn the destruction
> of those who seek to hurt us.

May we live as people of promise,
> as faithful followers of Christ,
>> that we might be bound together in peace. Amen.

Thanksgiving and Communion

Invitation to the Offering (Exod 14, 15)

With hearts filled with singing, let us bring forth our gifts and offer our lives to Christ, that God might work miracles of hope through our giving and our living.

Offering Prayer (Exod 14, Rom 14)

Merciful God, transform our gifts
> into gifts of hope and joy
>> for a world acquainted with despair.

Receive our very lives,
> and fashion us into instruments of your grace,
>> that we may become love and laughter
>>> in places of sorrow and mourning.

Mold us into your people—
> a people of promise and hope,
> a people who live and die in the Lord.

Sending Forth

Benediction (Exod 14, Rom 14)
    Plunge into the waters unafraid,
        for God leads us forth.
    Walk straight ahead with purpose and passion,
        for Christ is our guide and guardian.
    Live as people of powerful hope,
        for the Spirit renews us each and every day.
    Go with the blessings of God.

September 24, 2017

Sixteenth Sunday after Pentecost, Proper 20
Mary J. Scifres

Color

Green

Scripture Readings

Exodus 16:2-15; Psalm 105:1-6, 37-45; Philippians 1:21-30; Matthew 20:1-16

Theme Ideas

Living for Christ sounds so simple, but the reality is rather challenging. The Israelites grumbled, even as God provided for their every need; Paul glorified the idea of death, even as God called him to continue living and teaching the gospel. Like the workers in today's parable, most church employees would gripe if the last person hired got the biggest raise. And so, today's scriptures call us to remember everything we have received—the blessings of our lives, and the many miracles of God. In remembering, we discover gratitude and reclaim our purpose to live for Christ and to answer God's call.

Invitation and Gathering

Centering Words (Phil 1)

Come together as the Spirit calls. Love one another in the grace of Christ. Live together as the children of God.

Call to Worship (Ps 105)

Give thanks to God and call on Christ's name.
We proclaim God's grace and sing God's praise.
Seek the Lord, who is here with us now.
We rejoice in God's glory and strength.

Opening Prayer (Exod 16, Ps 105, Phil 1)

Mighty God, we thank you
for your wondrous gifts
and your constant love.
Guide us on the journey of faith,
and feed us with your sustaining grace.
Live in us this day,
that we might live in you
and answer your call.
In Christ's holy name, we pray. Amen.

Proclamation and Response

Call to Confession (Ps 105)

Seek Christ and the strength of God's love, for this love brings us mercy and grace.

Prayer of Confession (Exod 16, Ps 105, Phil 1, Matt 20)

Sustainer God, you nourish us in every way.
Forgive us when we reject your love and care.
Open our eyes when we neglect your gifts
and ignore your presence.

Draw close to us,
>that we may recognize your abiding presence
>>and guiding love.
Reclaim us as your own,
>that we might live for Christ
>>and answer his call of discipleship.
In the name of the living Christ, we pray. Amen.

Words of Assurance (Ps 105)

The living water of Christ rushes into our lives,
>bringing mercy and grace.
In this living water, we are washed clean and made whole;
>we are forgiven and reclaimed by God!

Passing the Peace of Christ (Phil 1)

United in the Spirit of God and in the mind of Christ, let
us share signs of peace and love with one another.

Introduction to the Word (Ps 105)

May our hearts rejoice, as we recall God's deeds in the
reading of God's Holy Word.

Response to the Word (Exod 16, Ps 105, Phil 1, Matt 20)

When God gives us food and we share with others,
>**we give thanks for our daily bread.**
When Christ calls and we answer yes,
>**God's will is fulfilled in our lives.**
When God rewards the least with abundance for all,
>**God's kingdom comes to earth.**
When we remember God's deeds
with thanksgiving and praise,
>**we sing with joy of God's power and glory.**
When we live to serve Christ,
>**we prepare the heavenly banquet table**
>**where all are welcome.**

Thanksgiving and Communion

Offering Prayer (Exod 16, Matt 20)
> Generous God, thank you for showering us
> > with your abundance and your love.
> Bless the gifts we bring before you now,
> > that they may shower others
> > > with your abundance and your love.
> In your generous love, we pray. Amen.

Invitation to Communion (Exod 16, Ps 105)
> Bread for each day, manna in the wilderness,
> > these are the gifts of God.
> Strength for the journey, water in the desert,
> > these are the blessings of Christ.
> Come to the table, and eat your fill.
> Christ's love will sustain us all.

Sending Forth

Benediction (Phil 1)
> Live as Christ in all that you say.
> Love as Christ in all that you do.
> Go forth as the children of God.

October 1, 2017

Seventeenth Sunday after Pentecost, Proper 21; World Communion Sunday
Deborah Sokolove

Color

Green

Scripture Readings

Exodus 17:1-7; Psalm 78:1-4, 12-16; Philippians 2:1-13; Matthew 21:23-32

Theme Ideas

God works in us, around us, among us, and through us. When we believe the evidence of God's presence in our lives, and when we surrender to the will of God for our lives, we become agents of God's redeeming love.

Invitation and Gathering

Centering Words (Exod 17, Ps 78, Phil 2, Matt 21)
The Holy One is always with us, in every place and time, working through us, and around us and in us.

Call to Worship (Exod 17, Ps 78, Phil 2, Matt 21)
Long ago, God led the Israelites through the desert—
by fiery pillar at night, and by cloud during the day.

We come to worship today, searching for God,
wondering if the Holy One is among us or not.
God split the rocks open in the wilderness,
causing water to flow down like rivers
to save the people from thirst.
We come hungry and thirsty for compassion,
wondering if anyone cares about our lives.
Jesus said that outcasts and sinners
would be welcome in heaven,
because they believe the good news of God's love.
We come today, longing to believe.

Opening Prayer (Exod 17, Phil 2, Matt 21)
Holy Giver of life and love,
you work in us and around us and through us.
As you travelled among the Israelites
on their way from slavery to freedom,
you gave them water from the rock
when they were thirsty.
As you walked among the people in Jerusalem,
you healed the sick and taught through parables
and stories.
As you move in and through our worship today,
you offer yourself to us and to all the world.
Unite us in love and service,
that we may bless the world in the name of Jesus,
who teaches us what it means
to do your will. **Amen.**

Proclamation and Response

Prayer of Confession (Phil 2, Matt 21)
Holy Teacher of humility and grace,
you emptied yourself of divinity,

and came to live among us
as a simple, human being.
Forgive us, Holy One,
when we take pride in our accomplishments,
and look for applause and praise
from those around us.
You walked among us healing and telling stories,
pouring out your life for the sake of those in need.
Forgive us, Gentle Servant,
when we guard our time and our money,
afraid that someone will take advantage
of our good nature.
You ask us to do your work
and to be the living body of Christ
for the sake of a hurting, broken world.
Forgive us, Gracious God,
when we focus all our time and effort
on what will please ourselves.

Words of Assurance (Exod 17, Ps 78)
The Spirit of God works within us
and around us and through us.
God gives us water when we are thirsty,
and rest when we are weary.
In the name of Christ, we are forgiven. **Amen.**

Passing the Peace of Christ (Phil 2)
As God is at work in us, we offer God's peace and grace
to one another.
The peace of Christ be with you.
The peace of Christ be with you always.

Response to the Word (Exod 17, Phil 2)
Holy Guide, you teach us how to live
and survive the wilderness of our lives.

**The mind of Christ lives in us,
filling us with love and compassion
for a world wandering in the wilderness.**

Thanksgiving and Communion

Offering Prayer (Phil 2, Matt 21)
　In humility and obedience,
　　we offer these gifts
　　　as signs of our willingness
　　　　to do your will in all things. **Amen.**

Great Thanksgiving
　Christ be with you.
　And also with you.
　Lift up your hearts.
　We lift them up to God.
　Let us give our thanks to the Holy One.
　It is right to give our thanks and praise.
　It is a right, good, and a joyful thing,
　　always and everywhere, to give our thanks to you,
　　who brought the Israelites from slavery to freedom,
　　giving them water from the rock
　　and leading them through the wilderness.
　We give thanks for your presence among us—
　　flickering like fire in the changing colors of leaves,
　　glimmering like golden carp
　　gliding below the surface of a stream,
　　fluttering like doves in the beating of our hearts.
　We give thanks for the life, death,
　　and resurrection of Jesus,
　　who taught us to live for the sake of others,
　　and to put aside all thought of personal gain
　　and earthly prestige.

And so, with your creatures on earth
and all the heavenly chorus, we praise your name
and join their unending hymn:
Holy, holy, holy Lord, God of power and might,
heaven and earth are full of your glory.
Hosanna in the highest. Blessed is the one
who comes in the name of the Lord.
Hosanna in the highest.
Holy are you, and holy is your son, Jesus,
who emptied himself of divinity
and walked among us,
teaching and healing and giving himself up
for the healing of the world.
On the night in which he gave himself up,
Jesus took bread, gave thanks to you,
broke the bread, and gave it to the disciples, saying:
"Take, eat; this is my body, which is given for you.
Do this in remembrance of me."
When the supper was over, Jesus took the cup,
offered thanks and gave it to the disciples, saying:
"Drink from this, all of you;
this is my life in the new covenant,
poured out for you and for many,
for the forgiveness of sins.
Do this, as often as you drink it,
in remembrance of me."
And so, in remembrance of your mighty acts
in Jesus Christ, we proclaim the mystery of faith.
Christ has died.
Christ is risen.
Christ will come again.

Pour out your Holy Spirit on us,
and on these gifts of bread and wine.
Make them be for us the body and blood of Christ,
that we may be the body of Christ,
present with Christ's love for the world.
God of water and wilderness,
God of clouds and rocks and fire and smoke,
God of humility and compassion,
we praise and thank you
for all that you have done. **Amen**.

Sending Forth

Benediction (Phil 2, Matt 21)
No longer outcasts and sinners,
but children of the living God,
let us pour out our lives like living streams.
May we fill the world with the water of your grace,
spreading the good news of God's love
in the name of Christ,
who is ever at work in us.

October 8, 2017

Eighteenth Sunday after Pentecost, Proper 22
Rebecca J. Kruger Gaudino

Color

Green

Scripture Readings

Exodus 20:1-4, 7-9, 12-20; Psalm 19; Philippians 3:4b-14;
Matthew 21:33-46

Theme Ideas

The readings today show us two different households.
The Exodus reading refers to Egypt and "the house of
slavery" (20:2), which threatened the people's well-being, joy, and hope. Set against this house, was "the house
of God." While demanding in its own way, the house of
God safeguards the family as it enlivens, gladdens, and
enlighten its members. Paul points to Jesus Christ as *the*
example of righteousness, as *the* one who has shown us
how to faithfully live out God's desires and will. When
we follow Jesus in every aspect of our lives, we know
the reward or sweetness of answering what Paul calls
"the prize of God's upward call in Christ Jesus" (Phil
3:14). In which household are we members?

Invitation and Gathering

Centering Words (Exod 20, Ps 19)

Long ago, our sovereign God brought the Israelite slaves out of the house of bondage. Today, do we dwell in a house of defeat and despair, or do we dwell with our redeemer and liberator in a house of freedom?

Call to Worship (Ps 19)

Brothers and sisters, we come from many houses.
Welcome to this household, the house of God.
Here we hear words that revive.
Here we experience grace
that makes our heart glad.
God offers light to our eyes.
Christ brings wisdom to our hearts and minds.
God's teachings are sweeter than honey—
even honey dripping off the honeycomb!
They are more precious than gold—
even tons of pure gold!
Brothers and sisters, welcome to the house of God!

Opening Prayer (Exod 20, Ps 19, Phil 3)

Teacher, Liberator, and Savior,
we are in awe of your glorious presence.
Your holy wisdom revives and enlightens us.
Your vast power releases slaves from captivity
and makes mountains smoke.
Your salvation comes in knowing Jesus Christ
and the power of his resurrection.
May our words and our meditations
be pleasing to you, awesome God,
our rock and our redeemer! Amen.

Proclamation and Response

Prayer of Confession (Ps 19, Phil 3)

Redeemer God, forgive our failings and our sins—
committed both knowingly and unknowingly.
May we not be ruled by sin,
and may it have no power over us.
Raise us from wrongdoing,
that we may share in the righteousness
of Jesus Christ. Amen.

Words of Assurance (Phil 3)

In the name of our Redeemer,
claim the righteousness of Jesus Christ as your own!
For in Christ, you are forgiven. Amen.

Passing the Peace of Christ (Phil 3)

Brothers and sisters, in the name of Jesus Christ, welcome one another to the household of God!

Introduction to the Word (Ps 19)

God's instruction is perfect, gladdening the heart, giving light to the eyes, and enlivening our very being!

Response to the Word (Exod 20, Ps 19, Phil 3)

Liberating God, too often we find ourselves living,
not in your house of freedom,
but in the house of slavery.
There we are trapped, ruled, and diminished
by oppression, addiction, and harm.
There we are robbed of our well-being,
joy, and hope.
Lead us out of the house of slavery
to your house of freedom.

Revive us and gladden our hearts
> in the power that brought forth the exodus
> > and the resurrection of Jesus Christ.

Thanksgiving and Communion

Invitation to the Offering (Exod 20, Ps 19, Phil 3)
Let us share the sweetness and preciousness of knowing a saving God by sharing our lives and our resources with others. With gratitude in our hearts, may we give generously this day.

Offering Prayer (Exod 20, Ps 19, Phil 3)
Loving God, we gather before you as a grateful people,
> but also as a longing people.
We see your hopes for us and for our world—
> hopes of freedom, gladness,
> > sweetness and righteousness—
> > > and we yearn to do our part.
May our lives and our gifts
> help to free people who are caught
> > in the house of slavery and dismay.
May our lives and our gifts
> help people find your house of love and hope.

Sending Forth

Benediction (Exod 20, Ps 19, Phil 3)
The Lord our God brought the Hebrew slaves
> out of Egypt and the house of slavery.
Jesus Christ arose in power
> over sin, death, and destruction.

Brothers and sisters, arise and break free
    from all that enslaves you,
    from the death that clings to you.
For you are members of the household of God—
    saved, righteous, and free.
Praise God, our rock and our redeemer!

October 15, 2017

Nineteenth Sunday after Pentecost, Proper 23
B. J. Beu

Color

Green

Scripture Readings

Exodus 32:1-14; Psalm 106:1-6, 19-23; Philippians 4:1-9; Matthew 22:1-14

Theme Ideas

We are to praise God and rejoice in the Lord always. The Hebrews of Exodus knew this, but with Moses taking so long coming down from the mountain of God, they decided new gods were in order. This was clearly not their best decision. The psalmist exhorts the people to praise the Lord because God is good. God's faithful love endures forever. Philippians exhorts the people to rejoice in God and be glad, focusing our thoughts and attentions on the things in this world that are good and honorable and just. Matthew's Gospel recounts a baffling tale of a king burning down the city of those who refuse to come to a royal wedding. The king then invites those on the highways and byways, only to toss out a conscripted guest for lacking proper wedding clothes. Unless you want to argue that the clothing is metaphorical for the virtues lifted up in Philippians, this passage stands alone.

Invitation and Gathering

Centering Words (Ps 106, Phil 4)
If anything is excellent…if any thought is admirable…if any course of action is holy and pure, righteous, and true…focus your mind on these things, and God will bring you peace.

Call to Worship (Phil 4)
Rejoice in God always! Again I say rejoice!
Rejoice in God's steadfast love.
Rejoice in Christ's enduring grace.
Rejoice in God's saving word.
Rejoice in the Spirit's gentle guidance.
Rejoice in God's healing presence.
Rejoice in God always! Again I say rejoice!

Opening Prayer (Ps 106, Phil 4)
Holy God, we come into your midst
    with praise on our lips
        and songs of joy in our hearts.
We come to stand firm in our conviction:
    that good is stronger than evil,
    that love is stronger than hate,
    that truth will ultimately win the day.
Keep our hearts focused on things
    that are worthy of praise,

and bless us with your peace—
a peace that passes all understanding.
Keep our minds grounded in Christ Jesus,
that we may know the joy of your justice
and your righteousness. Amen.

Proclamation and Response

Prayer of Confession (Exod 32, Phil 4)
Holy Presence, following you is seldom easy.
When we become afraid,
we allow our worries and doubts
to cloud our vision and obscure our faith.
When you seem far away,
we replace you with hobbies and work,
with desirable playthings and pursuits
that leave us feeling hollow and empty.
Forgive us.
Focus our hearts and minds
on things that are excellent, admirable,
and worthy of praise.
Shine the light of your love in our lives,
that we may see within ourselves
the things that are just, righteous,
and true. Amen.

Words of Assurance (Phil 4)
The peace of God, which surpasses all understanding,
is ours through Christ Jesus.
In Christ, we rest secure.

Passing the Peace of Christ (Phil 4)
When we keep our hearts and minds focused on things
that are excellent and admirable, God blesses us with a

peace that passes all understanding. Let us share signs of this peace with one another this day.

Invitation to the Word (Phil 4)

As we listen for the word of God, let us focus our hearts and minds on whatever is honorable and true, just and pure, pleasing and commendable, excellent and worthy of praise.

Response to the Word (Phil 4)

Bathe us in your compassion and love, Holy One.
Clothe us in your justice and righteousness.
Dress us in your mercy and grace,
> that our hearts and minds may be kept safe,
> > in Christ Jesus,
> > > and that we may find peace. Amen.

Thanksgiving and Communion

Invitation to the Offering (Ps 106)

God's steadfast love endures forever. As recipients of God's love and grace, let us show our gratitude for the many blessings we have received from God's hand by giving of our tithes and offering.

Offering Prayer (Ps 106, Phil 4)

God of steadfast love, your bounty knows no bounds.
For the abundant gifts in our lives,
> we thank you.
For the peace that passes all understanding,
> we praise you.
For keeping our hearts and minds in Christ Jesus,
> we honor you.

Receive the gifts we bring you this day,
    and help us stay focused
        on things that are excellent and admirable,
            holy and just, righteous and pure. Amen.

Sending Forth

Benediction (Phil 4)
    May the peace of God,
        which surpasses all understanding,
        keep your hearts and minds in Christ Jesus,
        from this day forward and forevermore. Amen.

October 22, 2017

Twentieth Sunday after Pentecost. Proper 24
B. J. Beu

Color

Green

Scripture Readings

Exodus 33:12-23; Psalm 99; 1 Thessalonians 1:1-10; Matthew 22:15-22

Theme Ideas

The glory and power of God unites these readings. Moses yearns to know God more intimately and to behold God's glorious presence. The psalmist speaks of God enthroned with the cherubim and seraphim while the nations quake. Paul proclaims that the good news did not just come to the church with words, but with the power of the Holy Spirit. Finally, when Jesus was tested by the Pharisees, he made it clear that just as Caesar is due the coin he mints to his glory, God is due the honor and glory that belongs to God. We may not be able to see God face to face, but we can all seek God's glorious presence with thanksgiving and praise.

Invitation and Gathering

Centering Words (Exod 33, Ps 99, 1 Thess 1)

Be with us Holy One, and reveal to us your glorious presence. For we hear your call to be more than we have become, and we long to be inspired anew in your service.

Call to Worship (Exod 33, Ps 99, Matt 22)

Let the nations quake and the peoples tremble.
  God sits enthroned in the heavens,
  bringing justice and righteousness to all.
Let the mountains tremble and the seas roar.
  God's glory is stronger than the foundation
  of the earth.
Let the humble of heart seek the living God.
  God's goodness and mercy sustain the faithful
  in times of trial.
Come, let us worship the Lord.

Opening Prayer (Exod 33, 1 Thess 1)

Holy Presence, reveal to us your ways
    and bless us with your glory.
Hide us in the cleft of the rock,
      that we may behold your radiant presence
          as you pass before us.
Call us to bring your justice and mercy
      to a world torn by war and strife.
Inspire us to embody your word
      and to live as a holy people,
          as we seek to share your message of love
              through the power of your Holy Spirit.
Amen.

Proclamation and Response

Prayer of Confession (Exod 33, Matt 22)

Gracious and merciful God,
temper our certitude with humility and grace.
Forgive us when we test others
from a sense of our own self-righteousness.
Forgive us when we do not take the trouble
to discover our own errors.
Give us the heart of Moses,
who wanted simply to know your ways more clearly,
and to perceive your presence more nearly.
Open us to your gentle correction,
that we may truly bring your good news
to a world in need. Amen.

Words of Assurance (Exod 33, Ps 99)

When we call, God answers.
When we seek, we are sure to find.
Call to God and seek the Lord with your whole heart.
For you will find God's healing, forgiving presence.
Amen.

Passing the Peace of Christ (Matt 22)

When we give to God the things that belong to God, the
most wonderful sense of peace washes over us. Let us
share this moment of grace by seeing the image of God
in one another as we pass the peace of Christ today.

Response to the Word (1 Thess, Matt 22)

God of grace and glory,
bless our lives with your presence,
and lead our actions
through your abiding word;

bless our faith with your Spirit,
and help us be constant
in our prayers and devotions,
through Jesus Christ, our Lord. Amen.

Thanksgiving and Communion

Invitation to the Offering (Matt 22:21 NRSV)
Christ says, "Give to God the things that are God's." Yet everything we have, and everything we are, is a gift of God's grace. What response is commensurate with such a gift? Let us be generous, as we rejoice in our blessings.

Offering Prayer (1 Thess 1, Matt 22)
God of manifold blessings,
enrich the works of our hands
and magnify the offering of our hearts,
that we may speak your truth
and share your love with the world.
Accept and bless these gifts,
that they may be of use to those in need,
even as they are visible signs
of the honor that is your due. Amen.

Sending Forth

Benediction (1 Thess 1)
Strengthened by the presence of God,
we go forth in hope.
Guided by the teachings of Christ,
we go forth to serve.
Led by the power of the Holy Spirit,
we go forth to love.

October 29, 2017

Twenty-First Sunday after Pentecost, Proper 25; Reformation Sunday

B. J. Beu

Color

Green

Scripture Readings

Deuteronomy 34:1-12; Psalm 90:1-6, 13-17; 1 Thessalonians 2:1-8; Matthew 22:34-46

Theme Ideas

Good works are no guarantee of good fortune. God takes Moses up a mountain to see the promised land—a land Moses will never reach. The psalmist pleads with God to grant the people a year of blessing and peace for every year they have suffered evil. Paul brings the gospel to the Thessalonians despite his terrible treatment at Philippi. Despite seeking to teach us the ways of life, Jesus suffers question and scorn from those who seek to discredit him. And still, we are called to remain faithful, to love God and our neighbors as ourselves.

Invitation and Gathering

Centering Words (Matt 22)

Called to live; called to serve; called to be kingdom people: Let us love the Lord our God with all our heart, soul, strength, and mind. And let us love our neighbors as we love ourselves.

Call to Worship (Ps 90)

Turn to the Lord with yearning
and with hearts ready to serve.
May God turn our mourning into singing
and our sorrows into laughter.
Come before the Lord with hope and expectation.
May God turn our weeping into celebration
and our grief into shouts of joy .
Turn to the Lord with yearning
and with hearts ready to serve.

Opening Prayer (Ps 90)

Eternal Mystery,
before the mountains were brought forth,
and before you formed the earth and seas,
you are God.
You make us like grass,
which flourishes in the morning
and fades in the evening.
In the blink of an eye,
you turn us back to dust,
for a thousand years in your sight
are like a watch in the night.
Restore us with your blessings, O Lord,
and heal us with your favor.

Make our works prosper,
　　for we are your people,
　　　　and you are our God. Amen.

—Or—

Opening Prayer (Ps 90)

Have compassion on your servants, O God,
　　and satisfy us with your steadfast love.
Make your works known to us
　　and bless the works of our hands,
　　　　that your love may flow through us
　　　　　　like springs of living water.
Help us rejoice and be glad
　　all our days of our lives,
　　　　that we may love one another well. Amen.

Proclamation and Response

Prayer of Confession (Matt 22)

Eternal God, like a mighty glacier,
　　your love moves all that stands before it.
As we struggle to love our neighbors
　　as we love ourselves,
　　　　be patient with us.
For we bear deep wounds from offering love
　　to those who have hurt us.
Nurture us in your healing love,
　　that our fears may hold no sway over us,
　　　　through Jesus Christ, our Lord. Amen.

Words of Assurance (1 Thess 2)

We have been entrusted with God's commandment
　　to love as we have been loved.

In fulfilling the law of love,
    we fulfill the law and the prophets.
In fulfilling the law of love,
    we find forgiveness and peace.

Passing the Peace of Christ (1 Thess 2, Matt 22)
    Fulfilling the law of love heals and completes us. May we be healed and completed this day as we share the peace of Christ with one another.

Response to the Word (1 Thess 2)
    May the hearing of God's word not be in vain.
    May we have the courage to declare the gospel
        to a world in need of good news,
            even when we face opposition and derision
                for doing so.
    May we be as gentle in our instruction
        as a mother tenderly caring for her children.
    May we share the good news of Christ's love
        with a world in need of this love.

Thanksgiving and Communion

Offering Prayer (Matt 22:37-39 NRSV)
    We have heard what we must do:
        "You shall love the Lord your God
            with all your heart, and with all your soul,
            and with all your mind.
        And...you shall love your neighbor as yourself."
    May the offerings we bring this day
        be a sign of our commitment
            to be known by our love.
    Bless these offerings and our loving
        in your holy name, we pray. Amen.

Sending Forth

Benediction (Matt 22)

God's love sends us forth.
God's love sets us free.
God's love makes us whole.
God's love brings us hope.
Go with God's blessings;
go and bring healing to our world.

November 5, 2017

Twenty-second Sunday after Pentecost, Proper 26

Leigh Anne Taylor

Color

Green

Scripture Readings

Joshua 3:7-17; Psalm 107:1-7, 33-37; 1 Thessalonians 2:9-13; Matthew 23:1-12

Alternate Readings for All Saints' Day

Revelation 7:9-17; Psalm 34:1-10, 22; 1John 3:1-3; Matthew 5:1-12
(See online supplemental materials for a complete All Saints' Day entry.)

Theme Ideas

Jesus sums up a major theme of today's scriptures: "But the one who is greatest among you will be your servant. All who lift themselves up will be brought low. But all who make themselves low will be lifted up." (Matthew 23:11-12). Jesus scolds the scribes and Pharisees for forsaking servant ministry in favor of earthly recognition: the best seats in the synagogue, honor at banquets, and respect in the marketplace. Paul reminds the church at Thessalonica that those who brought them the gospel worked day and night on their behalf so as not to burden anyone. The psalmist describes the fate of the wicked and the righteous: the Lord turns the rivers of the wicked into parched ground, but transforms the deserts of the faithful into springs of water. Humility and gratitude for God's blessings lead to servant ministry and recognition of our dependence on God, on one another, and on God's good earth. *(B. J. Beu)*

Invitation and Gathering

Centering Words (Matt 23)
Those who lift themselves up will be brought low. But those who lower themselves will be lifted up. True greatness is found in the one who becomes a servant of others.

Call to Worship (Ps 107, Matt 23)
Come into the presence of God,
who provides everything we need.
God's faithful love lasts forever.
Let us praise the Lord,
who makes a way where there is no way.
God's faithful love lasts forever.
Follow the Shepherd, who leads us into life
in beloved community.
God's faithful love lasts forever.
Come and worship our loving, Triune God,
who calls us to live in God's glory.
God's faithful love lasts forever.

Opening Prayer (Josh 3, Ps 107, Matt 23)
> Loving God, when we wander off
> > into the wastelands of our lives,
> > > your faithful love rescues us
> > > > and welcomes us home.
> As your beloved children,
> > help us understand what it means to truly live
> > > by serving others. Amen.

Proclamation and Response

Prayer of Confession (Matt 23)
> Holy God, you promise us
> > that nothing can come between us
> > > and your saving love in Jesus Christ.
> We want to believe, O God;
> > help us understand our doubts.
> *(Silence)*
> We want to believe, O God;
> > help us overcome our unbelief.
> When we forget who and what you are to us,
> > forgive us and humble us, we pray,
> > > that we may touch your forgiveness and love.
> *(Silence)*
> Amen.

Words of Assurance (Ps 107)
> We are forgiven. Thanks be to God!
> > **God's faithful love lasts forever.**

Introduction to the Word (Josh 3)
> Beloved of God, come close and listen to the word of God.

Response to the Word (1 Thess 2)
> Holy Spirit, inspire our hearts and minds
>> to welcome and receive your good news.
> May it do its redeeming work in our lives. Amen

Thanksgiving and Communion

Invitation to the Offering (Ps 107, Matt 23)
> Sometimes we give so that we won't be a burden to others. Sometimes we give to ease the burdens of others. Sometimes we give for the sake of the hungry, the homeless, and the desperate. Let us give joyfully, because to give is to follow Christ.

Offering Prayer (Ps 107)
> Holy God, bless these gifts,
>> for your redeeming work in the world.
> With these gifts, relieve the burdens of the hungry,
>> the homeless and the desperate,
>>> for the glory of your reign here on earth. Amen.

Sending Forth

Benediction (1 Thess 2)
> Go into the world, in the strength of Christ,
>> to love and serve God and your neighbor.
> Go out in joy, and live lives worthy of the One
>> who calls us into God's kingdom and glory.

November 12, 2017

Twenty-third Sunday after Pentecost, Proper 27
B. J. Beu
[Copyright © 2016 by B. J. Beu. Used by permission.]

Color

Green

Scripture Readings

Joshua 24:1-3a, 14-25; Psalm 78:1-7; 1 Thessalonians 4:13-18; Matthew 25:1-13

Theme Ideas

Choices have consequences. Choosing to follow God changes everything. Choosing to share the wisdom of God's holy mystery with the next generation provides our children a chance at a real future. Choosing to remain vigilant keeps us ready for when the bridegroom appears. Today's scriptures remind us that we need persistence, patience, and faithfulness for the long haul. But first and foremost, they remind us that it all begins with a choice: Whom will we serve?

Invitation and Gathering

Centering Words (Josh 24, Ps 78)

We make a thousand decisions every day, but few seem of much consequence. What if we made one decision today that would make all the difference in the world? Choosing, this day, to follow God is that decision. Will we do it? Will we share this wisdom with our children? The choice is ours.

Call to Worship (Josh 24, Ps 78, 1 Thess 4)
The God of our ancestors has called us here.
We are witnesses.
The wisdom of the ages has called us here.
We are witnesses.
The choice to follow God has called us here.
We are witnesses.
The Lord of life has called us here.
We are witnesses.

Opening Prayer (Josh 24, Ps 78, Matt 25)
Promise of the ages,
we come to you this day
to choose the way you set before us.
Strengthen our convictions
and grant us patience in our waiting,
as we watch for signs
of your coming kingdom.
Help us teach our children your ways,
that we may pass on a better world
to the generations to come. Amen.

Proclamation and Response

Prayer of Confession (Josh 24, Matt 25)
When our courage wears thin, O God,
strengthen our resolve to choose you each day.
When we grow weary in our waiting,

steel us for the long watches of the night—
for we long to be found ready
when you appear in your glory.
Fill our lamps with your grace,
that we might share your light with our children
and with the generations that follow. Amen.

Words of Assurance (1 Thess 4:17 NRSV)
We worship a God of mercy and love.
Hold onto these words of hope:
"We will be with the Lord forever."
Thanks be to God.

Passing the Peace of Christ (Josh 24, Matt 25)
True peace is found when we choose life and follow
God. True wisdom is found when we choose to wait for
Christ, even when the hour is late. Turn to one another
and share the deep peace and healing wisdom found in
choosing God each and every day.

Introduction to the Word (Josh 24, Matt 25)
Listening for the word of God keeps our lamps lit and
our hearts ready.
Listen…hear…receive…choose to let God in.

Response to the Word (Josh 24, Ps 78, 1 Thess 4, Matt 25)
Have you made your choice?
Are you prepared for the journey?
We will walk with God.
We will choose hope over despair.
Have you embraced your choice?
Are you ready to share the lessons you have learned?
We will live our choice.
We will teach our children
the wisdom handed down of old.

Thanksgiving and Communion

Invitation to the Offering (Matt 25)

Whether they are wise or foolish, people need oil for
their lamps, food for their tables, and love for their lives.
Let us share the bounty we have received, that no one
may be left out alone in the dark.

Offering Prayer (Josh 24)

We dedicate these gifts to you, Eternal One,
    as symbols of our choice to follow you.
Receive these gifts of love
    as celebrations of your presence in our lives.
Hold us to our promises,
    that we might share your blessings
        and wisdom with the world. Amen.

Sending Forth

Benediction (Josh 24, Matt 25)

Choose God this day, and keep your lamps lit.
    We go with hearts ablaze with God's love.
Choose God this day, and shine with God's light.
    We go with lives kindled with the call to serve.
Choose God this day, and enter into fullness of life.
    We go to embrace the life we have received.

November 19, 2017

Twenty-fourth Sunday after Pentecost, Proper 28
Amy B. Hunter

Color

Green

Scripture Readings

Judges 4:1-7; Psalm 123; 1 Thessalonians 5:1-11; Matthew 25:14-30

Theme Ideas

What does it mean to have faith? In the book of Judges, God's people live in a continuous cycle of seeking God when they are in distress, only to turn away from God when they feel secure. In the epistle, Paul warns against the foolish belief that life can be safe and under control. In the Gospel, Jesus tells a story of someone so determined not to risk God's disappointment that he stashes God's gift away, making it as good as dead. Our human impulses toward ease, security, and safety fall far short of vibrant faith in a living God. True faith is full of profound trust, aligning ourselves with God, even when circumstances are distressing and full of risk.

Invitation and Gathering

Centering Words (Ps 123)

Turn to the Lord our God, our greatest good and our Living Source. Turn to the Lord with eyes full of wonder. Turn to our God and live.

Call to Worship (1 Thess 5, Matt 25)

God calls out: "Come and enter my joy!"
We gather in thankfulness this day,
as servants of God's blessings.
God calls out: "Come, stay awake and be alert!"
We gather in expectation this day,
as children of God's light and love.
God calls out: "Come and share in my happiness!"
We gather in faith this day
to worship our God.

Opening Prayer (Judg 4, Ps 123, 1 Thess 5, Matt 25)

Our Lord and our God, our Greatest Good
and our Living Source—
whether in safety or in risk,
whether the path is well lit or in shadow,
whether we encounter approval or face insult—
we look to you for guidance.
Some of us seek to understand death, loss,
and the suffering of our world.
Some of us seek mercy and rescue
from the misery we face.
Some of us seek to know what to do
with the many gifts you have given us.
Help us turn our eyes to you,
trusting that you will answer us

with your mercy, your salvation,
and your joy. **Amen.**

Proclamation and Response

Prayer of Confession (Judg 4, Ps 123, 1 Thess 5, Matt 25)
Merciful God, we are aware of the ways
our faith falls short.
In our pride, we wait too long to ask for your help.
In our self-absorption,
we ask that our will, not your will, be done.
Even when you rescue us from our misery,
we quickly return to our careless ways.
Aware of these failures,
we turn our eyes to you,
trusting in your love and mercy.

Words of Assurance (1 Thess 5)
Friends, you do not live in the night
or belong to the dark.
You have obtained life and salvation
through our Lord Jesus Christ.
In him, you belong to the day.

Passing the Peace of Christ (1 Thess 5)
As children of God's blessing and light, greet one another with the peace of Christ.

Introduction to the Word (1 Thess 5)
You, beloved, are not in darkness.
**We will hear God's word as children of light
and children of the day.**

Response to the Word (1 Thess 5)
Beloved, when we live in Christ, we dwell in his light
and not in darkness.

**Let us wake from our slumber
and walk in the light of Christ.
Hearing God's word,
may it move us to live aright.**

Thanksgiving and Communion

Invitation to the Offering (Matt 25)
One servant said to the master, "Sir, you gave me five thousand coins, and I have earned five thousand more." Another said, "Sir, you gave me two thousand coins, and I have earned two thousand more." When we receive God's gifts and then offer them back in gratitude, God responds with abundance. God invites us to offer our gifts to the world, trusting in God's unending generosity.

Offering Prayer (Matt 25)
Living Source of every blessing,
    the gifts you give us are not trinkets
        to be hidden away.
Use these gifts for your service,
    that the blessings we have received from your hand
        may increase as they go forth
            to bring grace to the world.
Make our hearts generous, we pray,
    for you have been generous with us.

Sending Forth

Benediction (1 Thess 5, Matt 25)
Go forth as children of light, as children of the day,

Go into the world, knowing that God's gifts
of faith, love, and hope shield you
as you share those gifts with others.
Beloved, go forth to share in God's joy.
Thanks be to God!

November 26, 2017

Reign of Christ/Christ the King
B. J. Beu

Color

White

Scripture Readings

Ezekiel 34:11-16, 20-24; Psalm 100; Ephesians 1:15-23;
Matthew 25:31-46

Alternate Readings for Thanksgiving

Deuteronomy 8:7-18; Psalm 65; 2 Corinthians 9:6-15;
Luke 17:11-19
*(See online supplemental materials for a complete Thanksgiv-
ing Day entry.)*

Theme Ideas

O to be sheep in God's fold. In Ezekiel, God promises
to bring in the scattered and the lost sheep, bind up the
wounds of the injured, and bring justice down upon the
fat sheep that have chased the weaker sheep away. It will
be God who does this, not some hireling. The psalmist

rejoices that we belong to God, our shepherd. In Ephesians, we are called to give thanks continually for the grace, light, and power that God has bestowed upon us through Christ, who is above every ruler on earth. Finally, Matthew's Gospel continues the judgment motif seen in Ezekiel, and reminds us that our actions have eternal consequences. Our shepherd is righteous and just, and if we wish to abide in God's favor, we are charged to feed the hungry, clothe the naked, visit the sick and imprisoned, and comfort those who mourn.

Invitation and Gathering

Centering Words (Ezek 34)

Christ, our shepherd, is ever on the lookout for the lost and scattered sheep of God's fold. Our shepherd leads us safely to green pastures and tends our wounds. But woe to the proud and haughty sheep that scare away the weak...for they will face the wrath of our shepherd, who loves with equity.

Call to Worship (Ps 100, Matt 25)

Enter God's gates with gladness.
   Enter God's courts with praise.
For we are God's people,
   the sheep of God's pasture.
Serve God with joyful hearts.
   Love God by showing justice and mercy.
Enter God's gates with gladness.
   Enter God's courts with praise.

Opening Prayer (Ezek 34, Eph 1, Matt 25)

Glorious God, enlighten our eyes

to behold the hope to which we are called
and the richness of our glorious inheritance
in Christ, our shepherd.
Reveal your ways to us
and help us understand our actions,
that we might bring your light to the world
in all that we say and in all that we do.
Bless this church with unity and strength
that it may be Christ for the world,
who rescues the perishing
and reclaims the lost and scattered. Amen.

Proclamation and Response

Prayer of Confession (Matt 25)
God of glory,
we do not always see your glory
in the world around us.
When we see a person in need,
it is not easy to look him in the eye.
When we hear a cry for help,
it is not easy to offer her quick assistance.
When we know of a lonely prisoner,
it is not easy to make that visit.
Forgive us when we fail to see you
in our everyday lives.
Forgive us when we are afraid to act,
afraid to care.
Encourage us, God of glory.
Help us see others with the eyes of compassion,
that we might be your loving presence
in the world. Amen.

—*Or*—

Prayer of Confession (Ezek 34, Matt 25)

Loving Shepherd, we have not always reached out
    to the lost and scattered sheep of your flock.
We praise you with our lips,
    while averting our eyes from the hungry
        and those who suffer
            from lack of shelter and warmth.
We lift up our eyes to the starry heavens,
    while turning our gaze from the homeless
        and those who cannot help themselves.
Help us see others with the eyes of our shepherd,
    that we might be your loving presence
        in the world. Amen.

Words of Assurance (Eph 1)

There is immeasurable greatness in the power of God
    for those who believe.
There is unquenchable fire in the hearts of believers
    for those who have tasted God's hope.
In the name of Christ Jesus, who brings fullness to all,
    you are forgiven.

Passing the Peace of Christ (Ezek 34, Eph 1)

God loves us with a tenderness that can heal the deepest
wounds in our souls. Christ offers us shelter in green
pastures and leads us beside still waters. The Spirit offers us a peace that passes all understanding. Let our
hearts rejoice this day, as we turn to our neighbors and
share the peace of our shepherd.

Invitation to the Word (Matt 25)

Listen, our shepherd is calling us here:
    to feed one another,
    to show compassion and love,

to offer comfort and mercy,
to give as freely as we have received.
Listen, our shepherd is calling.

Response to the Word (Matt 25)

Good Shepherd, we long to be people of compassion.
When we see a hungry child,
help us see your face.
When we see a woman in rags,
help us see your dirty hands and feet.
When we see a man sick or imprisoned,
help us see your need.
When we hear your people cry,
help us see your tears.
When we perceive mourning and loneliness,
help us perceive your presence,
that our eyes may be enlightened,
and our hearts of stone may be replaced
with hearts of flesh. Amen.

Thanksgiving and Communion

Invitation to the Offering (Ps 100, Matt 25)

Enter God's gates with thanksgiving. Enter God's courtyard with praise. As sheep of God's fold, we have received goodness and grace from God's hand. Let us
show our gratitude as we collect today's offering—an
offering that continues Christ's work of mercy and compassion for all of God's lambs.

Offering Prayer (Matt 25)

Gentle Shepherd, may the gifts we bring this day:
be nourishment for a hungry world,

be clothing and shelter for those in need,
be compassion for those who are hurting.
Bless these offerings,
that they may help those in need,
and that they may remind us
of who we are really helping.
With gratitude, we pray. Amen.

Sending Forth

Benediction (Ezek 34, Matt 25)
Seek the lost and heal the injured.
We will encourage the fainthearted
and strengthen the weak.
Seek justice, but love mercy.
We will share God's justice
through the grace of Christ's mercy.
Go with God.

—Or—

Benediction (Ps 100, Eph 1)
Leave this place with thankful hearts.
We will make a joyful noise to our God.
Bring shouts and laughter to the world.
We will sparkle with our eyes enlightened.
Proclaim the tender mercies of our God.
We will share the good news with all.

December 3, 2017

First Sunday of Advent

Mary J. Scifres

Color

Purple

Scripture Readings

Isaiah 64:1-9; Psalm 80:1-7, 17-19; 1 Corinthians 1:3-9; Mark 13:24-37

Theme Ideas

Pay attention! Christ may appear at any time. God's silence will end, bringing dramatic signs of God's presence in our midst. Watching, waiting, staying alert, and paying attention are the themes of this Sunday and of Advent in general. In Advent, we are reminded that Christ is coming, but also that God is already with us, having appeared in the birth of the Christ-child. Paul reminds the Corinthians that they have already been made rich through Christ. They have every gift they need and are simply to "wait for the Lord." Pay attention! God is working to form us in God's image, and to form this world into Christ's kingdom. Today's scriptures invite us to take the time to see the signs and accept the grace that is already transforming our lives.

Invitation and Gathering

Centering Words (Mark 13)

Pay attention! There's something happening here. God is speaking. Christ is coming. God is with us even now.

Call to Worship (Isa 64, Mark 13)

Watch and wait, Christ is coming soon.
Christ is with us now.
Look and see, God's creative power is close at hand.
God's power is with us here.
Stop and notice, God has a plan to form our lives anew.
God is re-creating us each and every day,
re-forming us in the image of love.

Opening Prayer (Isa 64)

Creator God, thank you for forming us in your image
at the day of our creation,
and for re-forming us anew
each and every day.
Help us be attentive to your presence.
Open our ears to hear you.
Open our eyes to see you.
Speak to our hearts and shine in our lives,
that your presence may shimmer in our lives
and that your love may emanate from us,
now and forevermore. Amen.

Proclamation and Response

Prayer of Confession (Isa 64, Ps 80)

When we turn away from you
or neglect your presence, O God,

don't rage against us
or turn away in silent wrath.
When we sin and fall short
of the people you would have us be,
don't hide your loving presence from us.
Speak to us anew,
that we may hear your voice
and notice your presence in our lives.
Shine upon us with your grace and mercy,
that we may return to you
and return to love.
In your mercy and grace, we pray. Amen.

Words of Assurance (1 Cor 1)
In Christ, we are made new and rich
in every grace needed to restore us
and make us whole.
In Christ, we are forgiven
and made blameless before God.
Praise God for this glorious gift!

Passing the Peace of Christ (1 Cor 1)
Confirm the good news in one another, by sharing signs
of grace and peace.

Introduction to the Word
Listen and learn, God is still speaking.
We will listen for the word of God.

Response to the Word (Isa 64, Ps 80, Mark 13)
We call out, and God listens.
God calls to us, and we will listen.
We look for God, and God is present.
God looks for us, and we will notice.

We yearn for God, and God yearns for us.
We are awake, ready to respond
as God shapes our lives and makes us whole.

Thanksgiving and Communion

Offering Prayer (Ps 80)

Bless these gifts with your loving presence, O God.
Make your face shine through our offering this day.
Shine the light of your love
> through our ministries and our lives,
>> that all may know and notice that you are here,
>>> on this very earth and in our very lives.

Invitation to Communion (Ps 80)

You who have been fed with the bread of tears,
> find here the bread of life.
You who have drunk the sorrows of life,
> find here the living water,
>> springing forth with eternal grace.
You who need to see God,
> find here the very presence of Christ,
>> his life and love, ready to nourish us all.

Great Thanksgiving

The Lord be with you.
And also with you.
Lift up your hearts.
We lift them up to the Lord.
Let us give thanks to the Lord our God.
It is right to give our thanks and praise.
It is right, and a good and joyful thing,
> always and everywhere to give thanks to you,

Almighty God, creator of heaven and earth.
From everlasting to everlasting,
  you have revealed your mighty presence to us.
From the beginning,
  you have created and are creating,
  forming us anew, like clay
  in the hands of the potter.
When we withered like leaves,
  and floated away from your presence,
  you healed and restored us.
From ancient times, you have created us
  and called us to be your people,
  formed in your image
  and shimmering with your loving presence.
And so, with your people on earth,
  and all the company of heaven,
  we praise your name
  and join their unending hymn, saying:
  Holy, holy, holy Lord, God of power and might,
    heaven and earth are full of your glory.
  Hosanna in the highest! Blessed is the one
    who comes in the name of the Lord.
  Hosanna in the highest!
Holy are you and blessed is your holy name.
In the fullness of time, you sent your Son,
  Jesus Christ, to be present among us
  and to reveal your loving presence to us.
Through Christ's creative love and grace,
  we are formed anew and revived with your grace.
In covenant with you, we come—
  awake and alert, ready to know your presence
  at this holy table and in our very lives.

On that night before his death, Jesus took bread,
  gave thanks to you, broke the bread,
  gave it to the disciples, and said,
  "Take, eat; this is my body, which is given for you.
  Do this in remembrance of me."
When the supper was over, Jesus took the cup,
  gave thanks to you, gave it to the disciples,
  and said, "Drink from this, all of you;
  this is my life in the new covenant,
  poured out for you and for many
  for the forgiveness of sins.
  Do this, as often as you drink it,
  in remembrance of me."
And so, in remembrance of these,
  your mighty acts of love and grace,
  we offer ourselves in praise and thanksgiving,
  as children of your covenant,
  in union with Christ's love for us,
  as we proclaim the mystery of faith.
  Christ has died.
  Christ is risen.
  Christ will come again.

Communion Prayer
  Pour out your Holy Spirit upon us
    and upon these gifts of bread and wine.
  Make them be for us the presence of Christ,
    that we may be the body of Christ,
      revived by your grace
        and restored in your love.
  By your Spirit, make us one with Christ,
    one with each other,
      and one in ministry to all the world,

until Christ comes in final victory
and we feast at your heavenly banquet.
Through Jesus Christ,
with the Holy Spirit in your holy Church,
all honor and glory is yours, Almighty God,
both now and forever more. Amen.

Giving the Bread and Cup

*(The bread and wine are given to the people, with these or
other words of blessing.)*
The loving presence of Christ, shining in your life.

Sending Forth

Benediction (Mark 13)

Watch out.
God is all around!
Pay attention.
Christ is coming soon!
Wake up and notice.
Christ is with us even now!

December 10, 2017

Second Sunday of Advent

B. J. Beu

Color

Purple

Scripture Readings

Isaiah 40:1-11; Psalm 85:1-2, 8-13; 2 Peter 3:8-15a; Mark 1:1-8

Theme Ideas

Advent is a time of waiting and longing for the day of righteousness and salvation promised by God. We are called to wait with patience and perseverance, even as we look forward to the time when faithful love and truth shall meet, and when righteousness and peace shall kiss. In our waiting, and in our preparing to receive the long awaited one, these scriptures invite us to slow down, embody peace, and share comfort in an impatient and harried world.

Invitation and Gathering

Centering Words (Ps 85, 2 Pet 3, Mark 1)

Christmas is near at hand. But do we truly believe Christ is coming soon? Do we yearn for the day when faithful love and truth shall meet, when righteousness and peace shall kiss? Will we prepare our hearts to receive the coming miracle? It is time to get ready.

Call to Worship (Isa 40, Ps 85)

Look! Faithful love and truth have met in this place.
>**Righteousness and peace have kissed**
>**in our midst.**

Listen! God is speaking words of hope.
>**Christ is calling us into God's flock.**

See! The glory of God shines all around us.
The love of Christ flows through our lives.
>**Come! Let us worship.**

Opening Prayer (Isa 40, Mark 1)

Shepherding God, as lambs of your flock,
>we long to lie down in green pastures.

Lift us into your lap,
>and comfort our troubled minds.

Give us your rest,
>and strengthen our weary bodies.

Guide us through this season
>of anticipation and hope,
>>that we might lift our voices
>>>in laughter and song.

Make our paths straight,
>that we might move boldly forward
>>as we prepare for your arrival. Amen.

Proclamation and Response

Prayer of Confession (Isa 40, Ps 85)

God of shepherding love,
>we need your guidance this day.

You proclaim that faithful love and truth have met,
>   but we cannot see it.
You rejoice that righteousness and peace have kissed,
>   but we can scarcely believe it.
Forgive our jaded hearts,
>   and correct our wandering ways.
Breathe your grace into our lives,
>   and give us the confidence to shout
>   for all the world to hear:
>   "Here is our God!" Amen.

Words of Assurance (Isa 40)
>   "Comfort, O comfort, my people," says our God.
>   We have served our term.
>   Our penalty is paid in full.
>   Rejoice in the good news.

Passing the Peace of Christ (Ps 85)
>   In Christ, faithful love and truth have met; righteousness and peace have kissed. May we, who eagerly await his arrival, share the blessings of Christ as we share his peace with one another this day.

Introduction to the Word (Isa 40, Mark 1)
>   Prepare the way of the Lord.
>   Make straight the pathway for our God.
>   **Prepare the way of the Lord.**
>   Every valley will be raised up,
>   and every mountain will be brought low.
>   **Prepare the way of the Lord.**

Response to the Word (Isa 40, 2 Pet 3, Mark 1
>   Glorious God, source of our hope,
>   as we remember your promises of old,

help us live into your coming future;
as we reflect on the prophecies of advent,
help us prepare for the coming of Christ;
as we commit ourselves to the ways of peace,
help us find joy in the journey. Amen.

Thanksgiving and Communion

Invitation to the Offering (Isa 40)

Grass may wither, but God's word endures forever. Flowers may fade, but the promises of Christ abide. In offering our gifts to a world in need, we transform wealth that fades into an indestructible currency of God's love for the world. Let us give freely and joyfully in the spirit we find in Christ Jesus.

Offering Prayer

You have sheltered us in your flock, O God.
You have gathered us in your arms
and lifted us into your lap.
May the gifts we offer you this day,
reflect in some small measure,
the immense gratitude we feel
for the generosity of your love. Amen.

Sending Forth

Benediction (Ps 85, 2 Pet 3)

Christ is coming soon.
Love is on the way.
But Christ is already here.
And love is all around us.

Faithful love and truth have met.
    Righteousness and peace have kissed.
We wait for the fullness of God's kingdom.
    Christ is coming soon.
Love is on the way.

December 17, 2017

Third Sunday of Advent
Laura Jaquith Bartlett

Color

Purple

Scripture Readings

Isaiah 61:1-4, 8-11; Psalm 126; 1 Thessalonians 5:16-24;
John 1:6-8, 19-28

Theme Ideas

God's justice is a tricky concept for those who think
the status quo is just fine. These Sundays of Advent
are designed to prepare our hearts and our minds for
a new way of living in the world. God envisions an up-
side-down world, where those in power are suddenly
out of luck, and those on the margins are now the life of
the party. This is the world of which Mary will sing next
week. But for today, we see what it feels like to accept
God's call to be justice makers. If we are willing to both
embrace the vision and to work passionately toward its
fulfillment, we can be participants in the joy that God
seeks to bring to the world. And that will be a Christmas
worth celebrating! *(NOTE: Shirley Erena Murray's hymn,
"Star-Child," would be especially appropriate today.)*

Invitation and Gathering

Centering Words (Isa 61, Ps 126, 1 Thess 5, John 1)
God has a vision for a world with justice and joy for all.
Will we join in the dream? Will we rejoice with God?

Call to Worship (Isa 61, 1 Thess 5, John 1)
Rejoice always!
Rejoice in the One who loves justice.
Give thanks in all circumstances.
Give thanks to the One who loves justice.
Make straight the way of the Lord.
Prepare for the One who loves justice!

Opening Prayer (Isa 61, Ps 126, 1 Thess 5, John 1)
God of justice and joy, we gather together in your name
to proclaim the good news
of your presence among us.
Where there is oppression,
we will shout a message of your liberating love.
Where there is sorrow,
we will sing a song of your healing love.
And where there is fear, doubt, confusion, or anger,
we will shine the light of Jesus Christ,
your incarnate love,
in whose name we pray. Amen.

Proclamation and Response

Prayer of Confession (Isa 61, Ps 126, 1 Thess 5, John 1)
Merciful God, although we want to be people of justice,
**we are more comfortable with how things are
than with how things ought to be.**

Although we want to liberate the oppressed,
>   **we don't want to acknowledge our participation**
>   **in structures that oppress.**
And although we want to rejoice in the coming of Jesus,
>   **we would prefer that it not cramp**
>   **our already busy schedules.**
Forgive our reluctance to enter wholeheartedly
>   into the radical good news of your incarnation.
>   **Forgive us.**
Heal our pride, our need to be in control,
>   and our acceptance of the status quo.
>   **Heal us.**
Free us from the bonds of sorrow,
>   and turn our tears into prayers of thanksgiving.
>   **Free us.**
Transform our lives into a garden
>   where justice and joy grow
>   and bloom in abundance.
>   **Amen.**

Words of Assurance (1 Thess 5 NRSV)
>   The God of peace sanctifies you entirely,
>   keeping your spirit and soul and body blameless
>   at the coming of our Lord, Jesus Christ.
>   The one who calls you is faithful!

Response to the Word (Isa 61, 1 Thess 5, John 1)
>   *(This response is designed to be read by youth, along with an*
>   *adult worship leader. If presented with adult voices only, you*
>   *may want to tweak some of the phrases.*
>   Leader: The Lord has sent me to bring good news
>   to the oppressed.

Voice 1:	We bring good news when we construct health kits and flood buckets for disaster relief.
Voice 2:	We bring good news when we provide free child care to a young immigrant mother.
Leader:	For the Lord loves justice, and hates robbery and wrong-doing.
Voice 1:	We are God's justice-doers when we form friendships with special needs students.
Voice 2:	We are God's justice-doers when we refuse to allow bullying.
Leader:	There was a man sent from God, whose name was John. He himself was not the light, but he came to testify to the light.
Voice 1:	We testify to the light when we bring food for the food pantry.
Voice 2:	We testify to the light when we do yard work for an elderly neighbor.
Leader:	The Lord has done great things for us, and great is our joy.
All:	**We rejoice when we sing together of God's justice and love!**

(Ideally, move directly into a congregational song such as "For Everyone Born" (Shirley Erena Murray), "Joy to the World" (Isaac Watts), or "The Kingdom of God Is Justice and Joy" (Bryn Rees).)

Thanksgiving and Communion

Offering Prayer (Isa 61, Ps 126)
> O Lord, you have done great things for us.
> As we rejoice in your blessings,
>> let us also rejoice in the opportunity
>>> to spread your joy to others
>>>> through these offerings.
> May these gifts help transform our community
>> and our world.
> May they bring your kingdom of justice,
>> that we may all shout with joy! Amen.

Sending Forth

Benediction (Isa 61, Ps 126, 1 Thess 5, John 1)
(Ideally, this benediction would be led by two clergy or two worship leaders.)
The spirit of the Lord is upon each of us.
> **God is sending us to bring good news
> to the world.**
The light of the Lord shines upon each of us.
> **God is sending us to bring light to the world.**
The One who sends us is faithful,
and is with us always.
> **Rejoice always!**
> **Go joyfully to bring justice to the world!**

December 24, 2017

Fourth Sunday of Advent
Hans Holznagel

Color

Purple

Scripture Readings

2 Samuel 7:1-11, 16; Luke 1:47-55; Romans 16:25-27; Luke 1:26-38

Theme Ideas

If Christmas Eve tends toward the humble, earthy, and earthly—inn, stable, birth, simplicity—these lections for Advent's end emphasize the wild, eternal, and supernatural. A man, a woman, and an angel utter prophecies. Mary's *Magnificat* echoes Hannah's song of praise and predicts God's reign as if it has already happened. Grand mysteries, visions, and hopes are today's theme: ancient promise, royal lineage, power brought down, the poor lifted up, secrets revealed.

Invitation and Gathering

Centering Words (Luke 1)

Let those who ponder the last-minute gift, those perplexed by holiday details, those overshadowed in any

way—let them pause this hour, to see visions and hear
good news from far beyond our time and place.

Call to Worship (2 Sam 7, Luke 1, Rom 16)
May our souls magnify God.
May our spirits rejoice in God, our Savior.
God gives rest from all that afflicts us.
God goes with us wherever we go.
This is the God of mysteries,
of prophecies and promises.
**This is the God who lifts up the lowly
and fills the hungry with good things.**
May our souls magnify God.
May our spirits rejoice in God, our Savior.

Opening Prayer (2 Sam 7, Luke 1)
Before your Word becomes flesh, O God,
connect us with the wild, the ancient, the urgent.
Connect us to your words uttered in human voice,
from tent and tabernacle,
full of fear and mercy.
Connect us to your words uttered in angelic voice,
from the holy Name.
Attune our minds and hearts to you,
O God of mystery and greatness. Amen.

Proclamation and Response

Prayer of Confession (Luke 1)
We confess, O God,
that we expect no angel to speak to us.
If this is our greatest sin, we are grateful.
Make us ever more conscious

of how present you are with us—
present with us, yet far beyond us. Amen.

Words of Assurance (Luke 1:30-37 NRSV)
Mary said to the angel, "How can this be?"
The angel said, "Do not be afraid;...
nothing is impossible with God."
In God's boundless love, we are forgiven. Amen.

Response to the Word (Luke 1, Rom 16)
May your mercy, your mystery,
and your glory endure for ages to come, O God,
our wisdom and our strength. Amen.

Thanksgiving and Communion

Offering Prayer (Luke 1)
Mighty God, we offer these gifts
to fulfill the great works you do.
As you lift up the lowly,
as you fill the hungry
and fulfill your promises,
make us your servants—
servants who rejoice in your work. Amen.

Sending Forth

Benediction (Rom 16)
To God, who is able to strengthen you—
to the God of prophecy, wisdom,
mystery, and faith—
to this God be glory forever.
Go in peace. Amen.

December 24, 2017

Christmas Eve

B. J. Beu

Color

White

Scripture Readings

Isaiah 9:2-7; Psalm 96; Titus 2:11-14; Luke 2:1-20

Theme Ideas

This is a night for rejoicing—a night to sing a new song to God, a night to celebrate the salvation brought through the birth of Jesus, a night to embrace the light that shines in the darkness. God's light and salvation shines forth through a child who will rule with justice and righteousness. This is night to sing with all creation the glorious salvation of our God.

Invitation and Gathering

Centering Words (Isa 9, Luke 2)
All nights can look the same . . . if we don't know how to look. Jesus was born on a night not unlike this one. Love

took flesh in the watches of the night. The light of that birth continues to shine in the darkness. All nights can look the same...if we don't know how to look. What do we see on this night?

Call to Worship (Isa 9, Ps 96)

The people who walked in darkness
have seen a great light.
Those who lived in a land of deep darkness,
on them light has shined.
We are that people.
Christ is that light.
For a child has been born for us.
God's own Son has been given to us.
He is called Wonderful Counselor,
Mighty God, Everlasting Father,
Prince of Peace.
His authority shall grow continually,
and there shall be endless peace
through his glorious reign.
Let the trees of the forest shout for joy.
Let heaven and nature sing.
(Follow with the hymn, "Joy to the World")

Opening Prayer (Isa 9, Luke 2)

Holy and glorious One,
we have come to sing our praise
with the trees and the forests
for the birth of your Son this night.
As the earth rejoices,
let all people shed tears of joy,
for Christ judges the world with righteousness
and the peoples with truth.

We offer our thanksgiving for the child who leads us—
our Wonderful Counselor and Prince of Peace. Amen.

Proclamation and Response

Prayer of Confession (Ps 96, Isa 9)
We are not always prepared, O God,
to receive the Christ child into our hearts.
We do not always look to see your light
shining in the darkness of our world.
We are reluctant to leave our flocks behind
and search for the glory you reveal.
Overcome our fear, Holy One,
and inspire us to sing with the heavenly host
as we seek the Christ child this night.
Prepare our hearts, O God,
to behold your precious gift
in awe and wonder. Amen.

Assurance of Pardon (Ps 96)
Christ establishes justice and righteousness,
bestowing upon all people the blessings of peace.
Rejoice in the blessings of God's holy child.

Passing the Peace of Christ (Luke 2)
On Jesus' birthday, the angels appeared to the shepherds, proclaiming: "Glory to God in the highest heaven, and on earth peace and goodwill to all!" As we celebrate his holy birth, let us proclaim glory to God as we share the peace of Christ with those around us.

Christmas Eve Litany (Luke 2)
In the midst of a silent night sky, a star beckons:
Rise up, seekers, and follow.

In the midst of a tranquil field, an angel proclaims:
Rise up, shepherds, and follow.
In the midst of our loneliness and pain, God calls:
Rise up, children, and follow.
With the promise of new life, Christ whispers:
Rise up, beloved, and follow.

Response to the Word (Luke 2)
There was no room at the inn for Mary and Joseph.
Is there room in our hearts?
There was wonder at the angels' announcement.
Is there wonder in our hearts?
There was joy in Mary's heart as she beheld her son.
Is there joy in our hearts?
May it be so, O God.
May it be so.

Thanksgiving and Communion

Call to the Offering (Luke 2, Matt 2)
What greater gift could we receive
than the gift of God's own child—
a child who is our light and our salvation.
We, who have received so much,
are called to join the shepherds
in sharing our joy;
we are challenged to join the magi,
in offering our gifts to the Christ child.
Come! Let us give out of our abundance.

Offering Prayer (Isa 9)
Light of light, and Love of love,
shine through our offering this night,

that the world may be filled with your light
and be touched by your love.
Join our hearts to the joy of the angels and shepherds,
as we offer you our deepest gratitude
for the blessings of your Son,
the Prince of Peace. Amen.

Sending Forth

Benediction (Isa 9, Titus 2)
Once we walked in darkness.
Now we walk in the light of Christ.
Once we had no one to lead us.
Now we follow the Prince of Peace
who establishes justice in the land.
Once we strained to hear the harmony of your creation.
Now we hear the music of the angelic chorus,
and sing our praises with the trees and forests.
Once we were no people.
Now we are your people—
children with Christ, born of your glorious love.

December 31, 2017

First Sunday after Christmas

Mary J. Scifres

Color

White

Scripture Readings

Isaiah 61:10–62:3; Psalm 148; Galatians 4:4-7; Luke 2:22-40

Alternate Readings for New Year's Eve/Day

Ecclesiastes 3:1-13; Psalm 8; Revelation 21:1-6a; Matthew 25:31-46

Theme Ideas

Joy emerges as a common theme in all of today's scripture readings. Isaiah rejoices in God's glorious victory. The psalmist calls for praise from every corner of creation. Galatians reminds us that because of Christ's incarnation, we are now sons and daughters of God. In our Gospel reading, Simeon and Anna, who awaited the Christ's arrival, praise God when they finally meet Jesus. This is a season of joy and praise.

Invitation and Gathering

Centering Words (Isa 61, Ps 148, Luke 2)
>Joy to the world! Christ has come and Christmas is here!
>Let all of creation sing praise to our God!

Call to Worship (Gal 4, Luke 2)
>Christ is born.
>>**Praise the Lord!**
>God has come to claim us as God's own children.
>>**Praise the Lord!**
>Love has given us this glorious gift.
>>**Praise the Lord!**

Opening Prayer (Gal 4, Luke 2)
>Abba, Father, Mother, God,
>>we come as your children this day.
>We celebrate your presence in our lives
>>and in our world.
>We rejoice in the gift of Christ Jesus,
>>who claims us as sisters and brothers.
>As we move into this new year,
>>send your Spirit to strengthen us,
>>>that we may grow in your wisdom
>>>and rest in your love.
>In Christ's holy name, we pray. Amen.

Proclamation and Response

Prayer of Confession (Gal 4, Luke 2)
>When our hearts are unsure,
>>give us joy.
>When we tire of waiting,
>>grant us patience.

When we forget to sing your praise,
    forgive our ingratitude.
In this holy season, send your holiness upon us,
    that we may rejoice
        as your sons and daughters,
            as brothers and sisters with Christ.
In your holy name, we pray. Amen.

Words of Assurance (Gal 4)

In Christ, we are made sons and daughters of God;
    we are given the gifts of forgiveness and grace.
Sing with joy for these glorious gifts!

Passing the Peace of Christ (Luke 2)

Rejoice in the peace of knowing Christ, as you share
Christ's peace with one another and with the world.

Introduction to the Word (Luke 2)

Are you eagerly anticipating the Holy Spirit?
Are you prayerfully awaiting God's holy word?
Center yourselves: waiting, anticipating,
    and listening for the word of God.

Response to the Word (Isa 61, Luke 2)

When God's gifts are given, will you keep silent?
    We will laugh and shout for joy!
When God is present, will you keep your mouth shut?
    We will sing and dance with joy!
When love calls you forth, will you sit quietly still?
    We will go forth with shouts of joy!

Thanksgiving and Communion

Invitation to the Offering (Luke 2)

Bring your gifts in dedication to God. Bring your hearts
filled with love for God's world. Bring your whole

278

selves, that the Holy Spirit might bless you and bless
your gifts.

Offering Prayer

Bless these gifts, Holy God,

that they may become signs of love and joy

during this holy Christmas season.

Sending Forth

Benediction (Luke 2)

Go forth in peace, the peace of Christ.

Go forth with joy, the joy of the season.

Go forth with love, the love of God.

Go forth to serve, led by the Spirit of God.

Contributors

Laura Jaquith Bartlett, an ordained minister of music and worship, lives and works at a United Methodist adult retreat center in the foothills of Oregon's Mt. Hood. She is the president of The Fellowship of United Methodists in Music & Worship Arts, and was the Worship and Music Director for the 2016 General Conference of The United Methodist Church.

B. J. Beu is senior pastor of Neighborhood Congregational Church in Laguna Beach, California. A graduate of Boston University and Pacific Lutheran University, Beu loves creative worship, preaching, spiritual formation, and advocating for peace and justice. Find out more at B. J.'s church website www.ncclaguna.org.

Mary Petrina Boyd is pastor of Langley United Methodist Church on Whidbey Island. She spends alternating summers working as an archaeologist in Jordan.

Mary Sue Brookshire is a United Church of Christ pastor in San Diego, California, which comes as a surprise to her on many levels.

Joanne Carlson Brown is a United Methodist minister serving Tibbetts UMC in West Seattle, Washington and lives with her wife, Christie, and Thistle, the Wonder Westie.

James Dollins is senior pastor of Anaheim United Methodist Church in California where he lives with his wife, Serena, and his sons, Forrest and Silas. He is a lover of music, intercultural ministries, and timeless biblical teachings.

Karin Ellis is a United Methodist pastor who lives with her husband and children in Tustin, California.

Safiyah Fosua is an elder in the Greater New Jersey Annual Conference of The UMC, currently serving as associate professor of Congregational Worship at Wesley Seminary, Marion, Indiana.

Rebecca J. Kruger Gaudino, an ordained minister in the United Church of Christ, teaches biblical studies and theology at the University of Portland in Oregon.

Hans Holznagel, an independent writer and consultant, has worked as a newspaper reporter, as chief operating officer of a theater, and as a staff member of the national ministries of the United Church of Christ in such areas as communications, mission education, administration, and fundraising. He and his wife, Kathy Harlow, belong to Archwood UCC in Cleveland, Ohio.

Amy B. Hunter is an Episcopal layperson with a love for the Word and a passion for Christian spiritual formation in community.

Mary J. Scifres serves as a consultant in church leadership, worship, and evangelism from her Laguna Beach home, where she and her spouse B. J. reside with their teenage son, Michael. Her books include the *United Methodist Music and Worship Planner, Just in Time Special Services,*

Prepare! and *Searching for Seekers*. Find out more at Mary's website, www.maryscifres.com

Deborah Sokolove is professor of Art and Worship at Wesley Theological Seminary where she also serves as the director of the Henry Luce III Center for the Arts and Religion.

Leigh Anne Taylor is the minister of music at Blacksburg United Methodist Church and lives with her family in the mountains of southwest Virginia. She has recently published a book that she co-wrote with her former husband the Rev. Joe Cobb, *Our Family Outing, A Memoir of Coming Out and Coming Through.*

Indexes

Page numbers in italics refer to the online-only material.

Scripture Index

Communion Liturgies

For download access to the online material, click on the link for *The Abingdon Worship Annual 2017* at http://abingdonpress.com/downloads, and when prompted, enter the password: worship2017.